Emmie Returns

*For Darren Hovey
with my best wishes!
Liz Woodburn*

Emmie Returns

A Memoir of Two Lifetimes

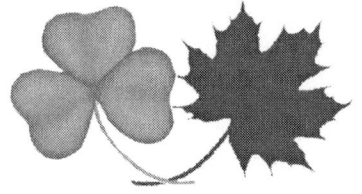

Liz Woodburn

ISBN-13- 978-1467959339
ISBN-10- 1467959332

Copyright © 2011 by Liz Woodburn

All rights reserved. No part of this publication may be reproduced, stored in a retrieval system or transmitted, in any form or by any means without the prior written permission of the author, except in the case of brief quotations embodied in reviews.

Cover photograph: Emmie Woodburn circa 1896
by Kellie & Co. Portraits
Cover design: by Jannine Cox

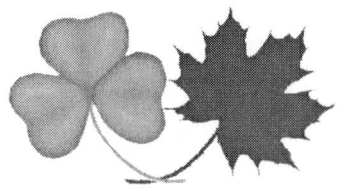

Dedicated to My Family

~~~~~

Contents

Preface i

Family Relationships Chart vii

1. Following In Emmie's Footsteps 1

2. Flashback To January 1897 17

3. Emmie Arrives In Ireland 39

4. Life In Limerick 57

5. On The Subject Of Men And Marriage 69

6. Diamond Jubilee Celebrations 85

7. Plotting Behind The Scenes 101

8. Emmie Longs To Go Home 125

9. Disaster Strikes 145

10. Back To The Future 163

11. Study Of Life And The Universe 175

Acknowledgements 203

Appendix A - Selected Bibliography 207

Connect With Me Online 213

About the Author 214

Preface

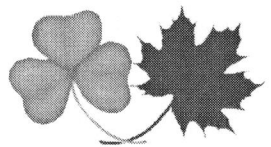

The origin of this story dates back to 1897, the year of Queen Victoria's Diamond Jubilee. My grandaunt, Miss Emily Woodburn, had undertaken a voyage from her home in Canada to visit relatives in Limerick, Ireland. While in Ireland, Emmie, as she was known, wrote an extensive series of letters to her family in Canada detailing the daily lives of the wealthy elite social class of Limerick. I inherited these letters from my grandfather who had been Emmie's youngest brother Ben.

Originally, I had considered that the story contained in the letters, merely offered a glimpse into the life of a distant relative. However, over time, I came to the conclusion that Emmie was more than just an ancestor. Through personal experiences that I deem to be aspects of 'Feminine Wisdom', I came to the realization that she was a former incarnation of mine. Over one hundred years after her death, I have retraced Emmie's footsteps on a parallel journey to Ireland and recognized our many temperamental similarities.

It has taken some work to get my head around being two apparently different people. My ego desperately clings to one single identity as well as the impossibility of existing in two different historical time zones simultaneously. I had to suspend much of my childhood teaching in order to reflect upon the issue of identity and time.

A prominent feature of my early childhood was the frequent and vivid dreams that seemed as though I'd suddenly woken up in another body in a completely different time and location. Usually these dreams had a nightmarish quality where I was in the midst of a frightening and gory scene of death. This could involve bleeding to death on a battlefield, being burnt in a fire, or drowning in icy waters. My senses were heightened as I heard the sounds of cannon fire and bagpipes, smelled the acrid odours of burning flesh, or felt the pain of frigid ocean temperatures.

Like most Western children I was taught to dismiss the content of these dreams as meaningless and worthless. Relating stories of invisible friends, talking to my dead grandmother, or 'having eerie feelings' were all met with disapproval and sometimes punishment. Like all children, I wanted love and approval so I learned to block out any experiences that did not jive with my family and community belief systems.

Furthermore, my education focused on the high value of technology and science. Subjects that employed rationality, mathematics, and the gathering of hard scientific evidence were highly encouraged and touted as the route to a successful career and a high-paying job. My emotion-based artistic abilities such as drawing, singing and dance were tolerated but only as hobbies that could never be relied upon to earn a living. This climate resulted in even greater practice at tuning out the 'female energy experiences' that bring wisdom and inner conviction.

I wrote *Emmie Returns* for two primary reasons. The first is to fulfill a promise made at Emmie's graveside that I would tell her story to the world. Secondly, this book is for the vast majority of ordinary people like me who have been taught that dreams, visions, and other 'feminine' ways of knowing are worthless and untrustworthy. I maintain that this stance results in loss of contact with important sources of Inner Wisdom.

An article in The New York Times of August 27, 2010 ("Remembrances of Lives Past" by Lisa Miller) indicates that one quarter of North Americans believe they have lived before. Currently there is a large body of excellent material available to the public on the topic of reincarnation. Many of the books on this subject have a 'masculine energy focus' on research, documentation, and logical attempts to prove that past lives have indeed occurred. However, the topic remains highly controversial. This is understandable when the majority of the population is unable to access actual memories that support a belief in reincarnation.

I have received a great deal of value from books about reincarnation that focus on documentation, research and an attempt to verify the validity of claims that people have lived other lifetimes. (Some of these books are listed in Appendix A.) I appreciate all the study and effort that has gone into the work of authors like Dr. Ian Stevenson, Jenny Cockell, Carol Bowman, Dr. Brian Weiss, Rabbi Yonasan Gershom, Bruce and Andrea Leininger and so many others. They have all paved the way towards elevating the topic of reincarnation from idle speculation to a topic worthy of careful consideration.

I believe that the time is ripe to look at the subject from a different angle. ***Emmie Returns*** approaches reincarnation from the standpoint of 'Inner Knowing', a 'feminine energy' point of view. Focus on external proofs has been suspended as readers are asked to reconsider their beliefs about the value of knowledge gained through 'feminine processes'. While the work of external authorities is certainly important, I assert that the modalities leading to individual 'Inner Knowing' are equally valid when considering whether or not we have lived before.

Regarding the structure of this book: the chronology of events has been deliberately mixed in order to demonstrate my own experiences in dealing with the issue of Time. The book commences in 2006 when I journeyed to Ireland, following in Emmie's footsteps. It was there that I realized through a mystical vision supported by numerous synchronicities that Emmie and I are one and the same soul. It was with certainty at Emmie's grave in Limerick that I made a promise to tell her story to the world, but it has also been difficult to simultaneously hold onto the notion of being two or more individuals.

During the five years following my trip to Ireland, my clarity was often sabotaged by self-doubt, distrust of my inner faculties, and fears of ridicule for asserting the value of knowledge that cannot be proven through traditional scientific means. I grappled with the meaning of my current life experience relative to Emmie's life decisions in 1897. What became evident is, that in spite of different outer worlds, we were plagued by the same inner conflicts and weaknesses.

Emmie's personal story existed within the context of her family as well as the confines of Victorian society. In later years her brother, Ben, confirmed that she had indeed been sent to Ireland to find a husband. Through limited surviving correspondence of other Irish relatives, I have been able to extrapolate and include the points of view of the main characters in the story. The politics of gender play an important role in the unfolding of events that occurred in 1897.

Integral to this book are my current investigations into issues of gender, power and how we must return to deal with unfinished business from the past. Through a mystical experience supported by uncanny synchronicities in Ireland, I received knowledge that satisfies me that Emmie and I are two aspects of the same soul. Yet it is entirely another matter to communicate this information to others who in many cases do not adhere to the same belief system.

My approach has therefore been to ask my readers to set aside judgment for the time being as I offer my personal story and thoughts about 'life and the universe'. Through comparing two lifetimes, my intention is to demonstrate how one individual soul progressed from the strictures of a male-dominated society to become a self-determined woman in the modern world. In no way does that mean I advocate female domination. In fact I see the world today needing to find balance in the expression of both masculine and feminine energies.

My personal experiences of past lives, both male and female, have all come through what I term as 'female energy modes' – dreams, deja vu, visions, synchronicities etc. Paradoxically, a large contributor to the eventual production of this book has been my training in the very masculine activity of martial arts. ***Emmie Returns*** asserts the value of balancing male and female energies no matter the gender of the body we happen to occupy.

~~~~~

Family Relationships Chart

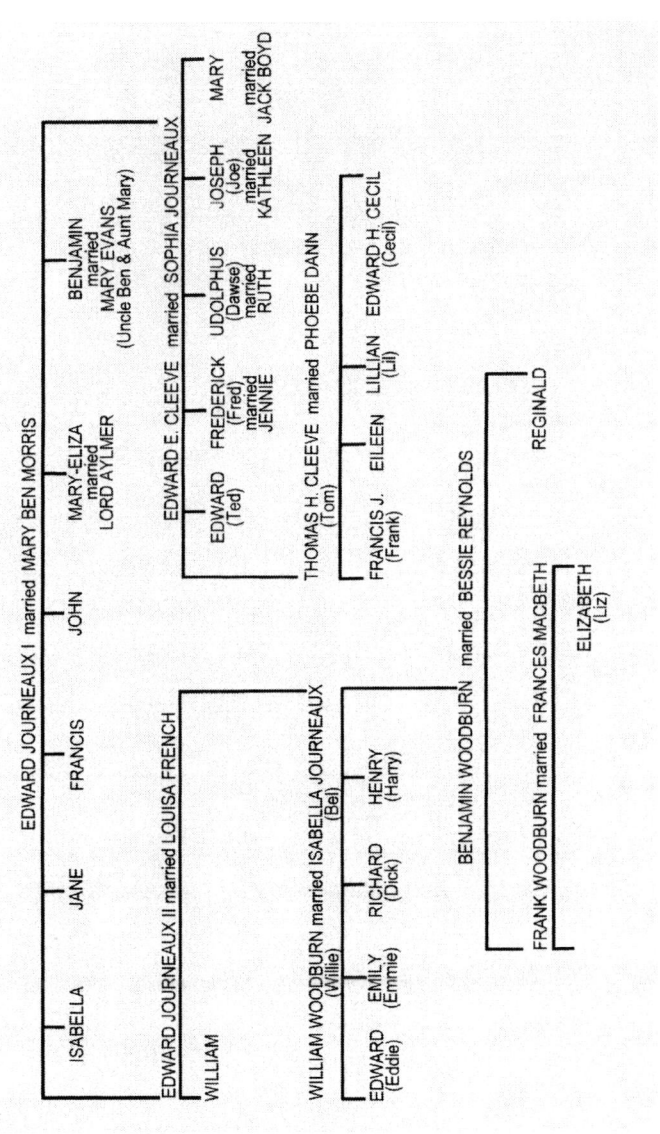

To view photographs of the main characters and scenes in 1897 Limerick, visit the Emmie Returns Companion Website at www.woodlandstream.com

ONE

Following In Emmie's Footsteps

The Journey Begins Again

Monday, November 6, 2006

Westminster Abbey, London

Standing before the tomb of one of the most famous women in history, I was overcome by a deep sense of awe. Right here before me lay the bones of Elizabeth I, Queen of England. How strange that her effigy in death brought her to life in my consciousness. In my mind's eye was the scene of a young woman defying tradition with her impassioned outcry: "I will have no man rule over me!"

I would love to have stayed longer at the Abbey to reflect on Elizabeth's success as 'The Virgin Queen.' But a quick glance at my watch told me that I had to make haste to catch a train. With my business in London almost concluded, I needed to turn my focus to the main purpose of this trip. For at long last the opportunity had arisen to follow the journey of a very ordinary woman in my family who also wanted no part of marriage. Alas, my grandaunt Emmie was never able to effectively voice her objections to that noble institution.

After catching the two o'clock train from Euston Station, my plan was to reach Holyhead on the Cornish coast in time to board the ferry bound for Dublin. I was so looking forward to retracing Emmie's footsteps on her journey to Ireland over a hundred years ago. Grateful for inheriting her letters describing that trip, I hoped to gain insight into Emmie's innermost thoughts and feelings through first hand experience on a parallel journey.

Logistics were working out well so far. I made it to the station just in time to pick up a lunch and board the train. After settling into a comfortable seat, there was now ample time to contemplate how far women have come in gaining the right to self-determination. In 1897 Emmie was subject to the need for chaperones on her journey. Today, I was free to go wherever I pleased without being accountable to anyone. The feeling of independence was delicious!

For her time, Emmie was doing well by undertaking an overseas voyage on her own as a young single woman. Yet she remained innocent of her family's agenda. I wondered if she would have consented to go at all if she had known she was expected to find a husband in Ireland. She was simply expecting a happy reunion with her cousins. With the benefit of hindsight, it saddened me to know that she was headed for a disaster.

There would be several other questions to answer on this trip. Visiting the hometown of my ancestors would indeed be interesting. I was very keen to see what had become of the fine homes in Limerick that Emmie had described in her letters. Would they still be standing? But more importantly, why was Emmie's story so compelling to me?

These were questions that would have to be answered another day. I was jolted from my reverie by the announcement that we would be arriving at Holyhead in ten minutes. It was time to re-focus, collect my bags and orient myself to an unfamiliar station. As it turned out, the ferry dock was quite a jaunt from the train platform. It made things easier to just follow the crowd that was headed to the HS Stena Line depot where the catamaran was docked.

The depot was rather bleak and the only restaurant uninviting, so I decided to venture outside to a small tourist bureau that sold the usual souvenirs. After purchasing a few post cards, I discovered there was a booking agent on hand that could reserve a room for the night in Dublin. I settled on a B&B, once called the Talbot, but now taken over by The Days Inn. It would be just a short walk from the Connolly Train Station and after a long day's trek, a cozy bed would be most welcome.

I returned to the depot just in time to hear the announcement over the loud speaker that the catamaran would soon be ready to board. Foot passengers passed through a thorough security inspection. My luggage went through the usual X-ray machine and I was frisked from head to toe. It was a female security guard who was most apologetic as she went through all my pockets and patted me down. While she went about her business, I stared at a glossy Stena line poster depicting the most up to date catamaran with the caption, "You'll fly there in half the time of a conventional ferry." This trip was to take one and a half hours. In 1897, Emmie crossed in ten hours on very rough seas. I was very grateful for fine weather and the wonders of modern technological progress!

After passing through security, I met up with a crowd of rowdy young people returning from a football match near London. There were also lots of families with young school children and quite a number of businessmen with their briefcases and laptops in tow. We took an escalator up to yet another waiting lounge with lots of large windows. I passed the time by watching a long line of cars inching down a road beside the pier, then disappearing into the hold on the lower level of the vessel. Eventually, there was an announcement that it was time to board.

This would be my first experience traveling on a catamaran. The interior was huge and resembled a giant shopping mall with high-end souvenir shops, gaming arcades, and fast food kiosks. Most of the passengers headed straight for a large dining area and formed several lines to obtain the Restaurant Special of the day. The most popular fare seemed to be a very generous lot of deep fried fish and chips served up with a large dollop of bright green mushy peas. I was suddenly nauseated. Not knowing what sort of sea legs I would have, I settled on a small plate of pasta with a pint of beer.

As the catamaran put out to sea, I found a quiet spot to settle down with my modest dinner. So far, the ride was smooth and I had no sign of seasickness. After supper, I was eager to watch the sunset through the vast glass windows at the front of the vessel. Soon enough, the lights on shore began to twinkle and we pulled in to dock at Dun Laoghaire. (Pronounced Din Learee by the locals) Relatively speaking, it was a short and easy journey- no ordeal of the rough seas and all-night chill that Emmie had to cope with in 1897.

After disembarking I was very pleased to set foot on Irish soil at last. Foreign nationals were required to pass through "Passport Control", the local version of Customs and Immigration. I was one of just a handful of people that were required to present their passport for stamping. Judging by the variety of different languages spoken, the bulk of passengers were European and with the new European Union, were permitted to just walk through. This was a considerable change from 1897 when Emmie's Irish-Canadian heritage allowed her to enter the country with ease.

The train station was just across the street from Customs. It was getting dark though and difficult to see where to go. I just followed the crowd to the station's entrance, purchased my ticket, for the first time with Euros, from a machine and located the platform for the DART (rapid transit train) into Dublin.

Dublin was in darkness when we arrived. My first impressions were that it was a rather rough and dirty place with the streets full of many smokers headed to the pubs for a pint or two after work. Talbot Street was easy to find and after a short walk I located The Days Inn.

At first it was difficult to identify the building. It was rather seedy looking and did not have the large bright signs I was accustomed to back home. The front door was locked and patrons were required to ring the bell to gain entrance. Grateful to have a place to rest after a long day's travel, I checked in and climbed the stairs to the second floor. My room was small but had a fabulous plush double bed with duvet and lots of pillows. After a long soothing hot shower, I collapsed on the bed feeling very pleased with myself for a successful day of travel that had gone off without a hitch.

First Day in Dublin

Tuesday, November 7th

Dublin, Ireland

I started the day with a full Irish breakfast in the hotel dining room, a rather modestly decorated spot, but offering a wide variety of hearty fare. By now, I had become accustomed to consuming a large breakfast to keep me going during a busy day of sightseeing and travel. Today's choice was sausage with grilled tomato, scrambled eggs, brown beans and toast with tea.

I had decided today to get a general sense of Dublin by taking the "Hop on Hop off" tour bus for a fee of fourteen Euros. It was a red double decker driven by a most personable guide who told all sorts of amusing stories of local history. My first stop was Trinity College, founded in 1591 by Queen Elizabeth I. The old cream stone buildings and cobbled quadrangles had once been home to such literary giants as Jonathan Swift, Bram Stoker, and Samuel Beckett.

Undoubtedly, the highlight of my tour at Trinity was the Book of Kells, a twelve hundred year old New Testament, hand copied and illustrated by Celtic monks. There was a fascinating video depicting how the monks created this manuscript, a testament to their faith and dedication!

It was not lost on me that, even in Emmie's day, higher

education was rarely open to women. My guidebook described Trinity as a place where "leading families sent their sons to be educated". Today, it was a relief to see the campus bustling with many women. I left Trinity College with a strong sense, bordering on smugness, that times had changed for the better.

My second stop of the day, The Dublin Tourism Centre, was located in a large old converted church on Suffolk Street. It crossed my mind that Emmie's contemporaries would have turned in their graves to see a stately place of worship converted into a commercial establishment. There was a brisk trade in souvenirs, a lunch counter, and a ticket agency offering discount packages for various tourist destinations. I was able to book a room at a Limerick B&B in preparation for my arrival there tomorrow. The tourist agent helped me with information on the local bus service to the suburb of Rathmines, my next destination. This is where Emmie had stayed with her Uncle Ben Journeaux upon her arrival in Ireland.

It was a little confusing to find the correct bus stop, but with assistance from some very friendly local people, I managed to find the Rathmines bus. What a delight it was to locate Palmerston Road and find the house still standing. Many of the old homes were still there, occupied by people who have sufficient money to refurbish them according to the standards of the National Heritage Trust.

No one was home at number 15. However, I did speak to a neighbour at the adjoining home, explaining who I was and that I was retracing the steps of an ancestor who had visited here in 1897. She was very kind and offered to take me on a tour of her home, explaining how their renovations were done in keeping with guidelines that maintain the historical authenticity of the building. It was a thrill to look out the windows and see the back gardens that Emmie had described in her letters to her parents.

My hostess explained to me that this housing development had been built under the direction of Joseph Plunkett, a prominent figure in Irish history. Charles Stuart Parnell, another significant politician, had also lived right next door to Emmie's uncle Benjamin Journeaux. I felt somewhat embarrassed not to be up on Irish history, but was very grateful for the tour and the information that gave more insight into my personal family history. My hostess suggested that I might like to see the local church that my family would have attended in 1897, so I made a point of stopping in after saying my good-byes.

It took some focus to retrace my steps to the bus stop. Fortunately, I caught sight of the familiar red double decker that would take me back into the centre of Dublin. By then I was getting tired and it had started to rain so I decided not to make any further stops. It was sufficient to get an overview of the city as we passed some of Dublin's more famous sites like the Guinness Brewery, Jameson's whiskey distillery, St. Patrick's Cathedral, and Temple Bar.

With the benefit of daylight, Dublin was starting to grow on me. My initial negative judgements had transformed into strong feelings of appreciation for this historic city. In spite of the fact that this was my first visit, I could not explain a rapidly growing sense of familiarity.

My final destination for the day was the General Post Office on O'Connell Street, scene of the Easter Rising of 1916. Some ninety years later, the walls were still pock-marked with bullet holes and the building was heavily protected by armed guards. As I posted some cards to friends back in Canada, I thought of the many struggles the Irish people had been through since Emmie's visit in 1897. Returning to my hotel in the drizzling rain, I was overcome with sadness for lives lost in the many human struggles to be free from patriarchal oppression. It was not lost on me however, that Emmie's family were Royalists and were not in favour of Home Rule.

What Was That?

Wednesday, November 9th

I woke up refreshed at eight o'clock and after packing my bags, went for breakfast. I had settled on taking the four o'clock train to Limerick from Heuston Station, the same station that Emmie had used in 1897. My main destination for the day was Joyce House, the registry office for Births, Marriages, and Deaths in Ireland.

It was on my to-do list to obtain a copy of Emmie's death registration for my genealogy records at home. After checking out of the hotel, I walked past The Custom House, crossed the famous river Liffy, and made my way to the General Register Office on Lombard Street. Finding Emmie's death registration turned out to be much simpler than I had expected. For a fee of two Euros, I was given a large bound index book for the appropriate year. The deaths were listed in alphabetical order and, after finding the registration number, I was able to order (for four Euros) a photocopy of the original document.

With my business concluded at the Registry office, there were three hours to fill before the departure of the train to Limerick. I was keen to tour the Kilmainham Gaol, an infamous prison that had been in use from 1792-1924. This site had been strongly recommended as 'a must-do' by friends back home. However, it was raining and I would have to store my bags in a locker at Heuston Station. Time would be tight.

I decided it would be worth pushing myself, thinking it may be some time before I get to Dublin again. I had a premonition that this would be an important mission. After all, Emmie's grandfather had been the jail-keeper in Limerick and her father had grown up in apartments adjoining the Limerick Jail. There was a family connection with jails.

Sure enough, the Kilmainham Gaol was an amazing place! True, it was a very sobering and sad place; a harsh, hard and nasty place. I felt great heaviness and sadness in the jail where even young children were jailed for petty offences like stealing a tulip or a spoon. During the Potato Famine, many women had been incarcerated there for stealing food to feed their starving children.

Joseph Plunkett, who had built the Palmerston Road houses I had seen yesterday, was incarcerated and executed at Kilmainham for his part in the 1916 Easter uprising. Charles Stuart Parnell, who lived next door to Emmie's Uncle Ben when he was in Dublin, was jailed there. While Parnell received preferential treatment due to his connection to Prime Minister Gladstone, most of the prisoners endured unimaginable hardship at Kilmainham.

I was horrified by the conditions. The cells were little more than animal pens, dark and damp and over-crowded. The people I had read about in the history books had actually been there-

Eamon de Valera, James Connolly and Joseph Plunkett. (Connolly was in such poor condition that he had to be tied to a chair before he was shot by firing squad.) The tour concluded with a visit to the Chapel where Joseph Plunkett had married Grace Gifford by candlelight just two hours before his execution.

I am so glad to have made the effort to visit this historic spot. In spite of the sombreness of the experience, I had a strong sense that it was an important part of Irish history and that one ought to experience it to get an understanding of the power struggles that have forged modern day Ireland. Later on, I considered that the tour of the Kilmainham Gaol was one of the highlights of my trip.

Perhaps it was the great emotion of this experience that opened me up to what was to occur next. In retrospect, I realize that the next few moments were vital to Emmie's story, even though so many years had passed since her death. For, Emmie had been in her own sort of prison along with the majority of women of her time. While the past could not be changed, it was time for liberation in the present!

Hurrying along a misty pathway to the train station through the grounds of the Museum of Art, I was glad that the rain had stopped. The wet grass was a vivid green in spite of a still cloudy sky. I was in a very pensive mood after my experience in the gaol, aware of a myriad of sympathetic feelings for all the suffering that had taken place there. Deeply engrossed in thought, I had a very odd sense that someone had come up behind me on the path. This 'Presence' spoke to me, saying "Good for you for pushing yourself to visit the gaol."

My knee-jerk response was, "Who are you and what do you want?"

The Presence answered, "I am Willie Woodburn, Emmie's father."

In that moment, I felt Emmie's great estrangement and coldness towards her father. A sudden surge of forceful energy overtook me as I launched into a loud and angry tirade:

"What you did was terribly wrong. It was wrong to force me into an unwanted marriage. It was very wrong to send me to Ireland under false pretenses. I had a right to know beforehand that you required me to find a husband and marry. I wanted no part of that. I had a right to choose the course of my life and if you had decided that you couldn't keep me, I could have managed quite well on my own."

Willie stubbornly held his ground, "I was the head of the household. You were my daughter. It was your duty to obey. It was my duty to protect you and provide for your future."

The anger rose in my throat, "Well I would rather die than be forced to marry against my will. How could you turn me out of the only home I knew? It broke my heart to be separated from those near and dear to me. I could have managed to make a life for myself in Canada without your meddling. Today I travel overseas all on my own. I have made all of my travel arrangements, earned my own money, and am managing just fine to go wherever I please without the need of any chaperone. You may think women are helpless and dependent on men, but we aren't. And I have proven it!"

At that point, there was no further reply. Willie had faded into thin mist and, as I glanced about, I felt great relief to realize that I was quite alone on the path. No one was around to have witnessed this apparently one-sided interchange. What had just happened here? For certainly SOMETHING had happened.

But what was it? It was as though I was both Emmie and Liz rolled into one. Was Emmie more than a distant relative? Is it possible that our common birthday was a clue? Had I just completed something that Emmie had been unable to do? This felt like a victory - not for someone else, but for me. I had stood up for myself. Had I given Emmie the voice she could not find so long ago? And was there some way that my voice was also her voice?

Jails Without Walls

I would have to address these questions later. Once again, my watch had taken on the role of 'master' and told me I'd better get a move-on. The Limerick train would be departing soon and there was still a lunch to purchase and luggage to retrieve from the station locker. Winded from my jog to Heuston Station, I arrived with a few minutes to spare. Emmie had arrived at this very location in 1897 via horse and buggy, accompanied by Cousin Phoebe and Uncle Ben. While the old station building was much the same, it was very evident from the jam of modern automobiles that so much had changed since then!

The Limerick train was already at the platform. It was half empty and I was glad to find a quiet spot to settle in and ponder my experience on the pathway from the Kilmainham Gaol. There was something delicious about my current feeling of independence and competence. It was as though I had been released from old ties of suppression and limitation, both now and in the past.

It was also curious that this feeling was connected to leaving a notorious old prison. I realized then that not all jails have walls.

Women have been imprisoned in limited societal roles for a very long time and still are in many cultures. A rush of gratitude for all the women who have fought for equality and the right to self-determination flushed over me. By giving Emmie a voice, I had come into my own. This was a most powerful feeling!

As the train pulled out of Heuston Station, I seemed to drift back and forth between the consciousness of Emmie in 1897 and of Liz in 2006. Over a hundred years ago when Emmie was on the train bound for Limerick, she was innocent of any ulterior motives on the part of her family and chaperones. No doubt, she thought of her parents back in Canada and looked forward to filling them in on all the details of her adventures. It was difficult not to worry about how they were getting on and impossible to imagine that she would never see them again.

As I contemplated the morning's experience of time warp in my encounter with Emmie's father, the crux of her conflict came to light. She knew she was a key support to her mother in coping with the endless list of "women's work" in a household full of males. On the other hand, her journey had exposed a keen sense of adventure and deep inner longing for independence. Emmie would have been happy to return to her family in Canada but she wanted no part of a marriage in Ireland. She was bound by duty but longed to follow her own heart.

From a father's point of view in 1897, it was a primary duty to protect his wife and especially his female children. In return, women had a duty to obey and that was that. What was there to question? After all, did not Willie Woodburn have his daughter's best interests at heart? As head of the household, of course he knew best what she must do to secure a happy future. Moreover, there would be no restful nights until this sacred duty was fulfilled.

~~~~~

Woodburn Family around 1889: Back row standing: Emmie age 16, brother Edward. Front row L to R: Harry, Willie Woodburn, Ben, Bel Woodburn, Dick.

TWO

Flashback To January 1897

Willie Woodburn Faces the Prospect of a Bleak Future

The winter of 1897 has brought hard times to the Woodburn family. Who would have ever thought that Willie Woodburn, proprietor of the Melbourne General Store, would be looking upon such a bleak future? There is no sense wallowing in regret for deciding to leave the stove on overnight in the store. Everyone knows it is indeed bitterly cold – the worst winter in years people are saying – and there was nothing else to do but try to keep some heat in the place. Yes, it's regrettable that the store has burnt to the ground, but the fault lies with those scoundrels at the insurance company for disputing the claim. All of the townspeople will attest to the fact that William John Woodburn is an honest and upstanding citizen and there is no reason whatsoever to suspect any sort of skullduggery.

This is most certainly a predicament to keep a man from his sleep at night. It appears that the insurance company is not about to settle any time soon. With no income and seven mouths to feed, something has got to be done. There is little hope of getting work in the dead of an Eastern Townships winter. At age fifty-three, Willie Woodburn is a little long in the tooth to expect anyone to hire him. Perhaps the two older boys, Eddie and Dick would have a chance of finding something, but they can hardly be expected to take on the load of supporting the entire family. Besides, a man's pride cannot allow things to come to such a degrading state.

Then there are Harry and Ben, the two younger boys, still in school. Perhaps the finances could be stretched to allow them to finish the Spring term. For God knows, boys have got to have an education if they are to make anything of themselves in this world. They could hire on as farm workers for the summer and get room and board to boot.

But what about Emmie? 'Tis a worry that at twenty-three years of age, my darling only daughter has shown no inclination to find herself a suitable husband. Soon it will be too late and how is she to be supported when her dear Dad is no longer around? Employment is out of the question for a well-bred young lady. Besides, she is a handsome woman – and well accomplished – perhaps there is no one good enough for her around these parts. Back home in Ireland, she'd have been snapped up long ago by some fine young man with only the best of prospects.

There is only one solution which I will put to my dear wife, Bel, in the morning. Emmie must be sent back to the Old Country on a husband-finding mission. Bel has fine family connections in Dublin and Limerick. True, Bel's mother's cousin, Lord Aylmer, is spending most of his time in Canada now and his wife Mary, has long been in her grave, but Aunt Sofia Cleeve could, no doubt, prevail upon her son, Thomas, to help out at the Limerick end.

Uncle Ben and Aunt Mary Journeaux would do their part on the Dublin social circuit. Hadn't they written to Bel recently that young Frank Cleeve was an eligible bachelor and very handsome too, and wouldn't Frank and Emily make a splendid couple? Yes, Emily's future must be secured and there is no better time than the present to secure it.

Well, that solves the biggest of my worries. Now I can get some sleep.

February 1897 – Willie Delights in a Family Conspiracy

Well now, that's done! This is indeed a satisfying day for Willie Woodburn. The morning's mail has brought a reply from Aunt Sofia Cleeve to Bel's letter last month detailing Emily's plight. Of course it took the suggestion of the Head of the Household – yours truly – to set things in motion, but women can be counted upon to run with it when it comes to affairs of the heart.

A plan has been concocted that Tom and Phoebe Cleeve will send Emmie an invitation (and the money for her passage) to join them in the Spring in Old Ireland for celebrations of Queen Victoria's Diamond Jubilee. Of course, the social circuit will be extra full due to said celebrations, affording many fine opportunities to meet eligible young men of the right sort.

No doubt, Emmie will get caught up in the tide of gayety and delight and she is bound to simply fall in love under the circumstances. To preserve her innocence and sense of delicacy, she need know nothing of the motives and machinations behind the scenes.

Our good friends, the Macys are going over at the end of April and have suggested that Emmie travel with them. That solves the problem of a young lady travelling alone. Cousin Dawse Cleeve will be available to meet her at Liverpool and get her safely across the Channel to Uncle Ben and Aunt Mary in Dublin. They are absolutely delighted at the news that dear Emmie is coming to visit and look forward to being collaborators in our "little project". Mind you, they are getting on in years and don't have so many connections with the young folk anymore. Chances are there will be better luck with the Cleeves once Emmie travels down to Limerick.

It seems the best route would be to take the train to Portland Maine and meet up with the ship on its way to Halifax. The Macys will come on board around the same time and the Macy girls, Sally and Ella, will be wonderful company for Emmie on the sea voyage. Captain Macy can be counted upon to be an outstanding chaperone.

March 1897 – Willie Solves a Problem

Still no prospect of work. It's looking like it will take a widening of the circle, perhaps as far as Ste. Hyacinthe to find something. The insurance company is still dragging its heels and there is no sign of any money from that direction. Eddie and Dick are looking for work in Montreal , but it is costing a pretty penny for their room and board in the mean time. Ben's eyes are giving him trouble and the doctor's bills are piling up. He and Harry will just have to pull out of school early and catch up next Fall. Hopefully, times will be better by then.

'Tis a relief that Emmie will soon be on her way to Ireland. She hasn't been very well lately with some sort of pain in her hip that recurs periodically. Must be "Women's Troubles" and that is Bel's domain. No sense in running up more doctor's bills only to find out that all the dear girl needs to set things right is to fulfill her natural function as a wife and mother. All the same, 'tis a worry. But the fresh sea air and Irish countryside will do her a world of good and she will be right as rain in no time.

Bel is putting together a "trousseau". Dear Emmie must be dressed to the nines if she is to attract the right sort of mate, and I wouldn't have it any other way. She is naturally handsome and ought to be gussied up to match. All the same, it's costing more than enough to buy the materials for new dresses. It's a good thing Bel is so handy with the needle and we don't have to buy 'ready-made'.

Emmie's passage is booked on the S.S. Vancouver. She'll leave from Sherbrooke by the overnight train on the twenty-eighth of April. After the ship leaves Portland, there will be an overnight stop in Halifax before they put out to sea, then a ten-day crossing, arriving in Liverpool around the ninth of May. These modern sailing vessels are a wonder! Why, I remember the crossing took twice as long when I came out from Ireland as a young man.

I shall miss the dear girl, but mustn't be selfish. It's a father's duty to see his daughter's future secured and I'll not shirk that responsibility. I do hope she doesn't decide to remain in Ireland once she's tied the knot. It would be a delight to grow old with dear Bel at my side and my grandchildren nearby. Of course the boys will settle down soon enough, but there's something special about hearing your daughter sing to her young ones,

> "Baby's eyes are Irish, Baby's eyes are blue,
> Baby's eyes are Daddy's eyes, just like Mother's too."

April 1897 – Emmie's Adventure Begins

S.S. Vancouver

April 30th 1897

My Dear Father, Mother, Harry & Ben,

We are far out from land. (No land in sight.) But the Captain says that if the fog would lift, we would see a thin line. It is nine o'clock. I have just finished breakfast (a good one) and as it is wet I thought I would remain below for a while.

Now I will tell you how I arrived so far. At Sherbrooke, as the train passed through, there was sign of daylight – I could see that the land was flooded badly, many houses being in water; this continued till we passed Norton Falls where part of the dam gave way, hiding fences etc. for many miles. At twenty minutes to five the lamps in the train were put out, at half past five we reached Island Pond, and a gentleman came in to see to our bags etc. He asked me so nicely if I had trunks and where bound for. I told him and he said I would have to get out and claim mine and see it put on board again. I told him I expected to see Mr. White as we had asked him to meet me. Why, said he, I am a great friend of his and work in the same office with Mr. Stolle and if you are not met I will see you through. In a little while this nice man, for he was so polite and kind, came in and took the number and my cheques as there was no sight of Mr. White, and a few minutes before we left he came again and said my trunks were safe on board. So I had no trouble and never left my seat until the Macy's came on at Yarmouth and received me with open arms.

Berlin Falls is such a stormy spot. I never saw such rocks. Behind the town is a regular mountain. All the way from here the seeing was lovely, though in many places the snow lay thick, but the country seemed full of pretty little winding brooks with several rivers, and in places grand hills. The passengers were a nasty rough lot, intermediators for this ship. There was no second-class car on till Island Pond where they were hurried out. Among eight people, two bottles of brandy were drunk between Richmond and where they left the car. Only when the conductor came in were they quiet- so I could not sleep and by the time I got to Portland my head ached badly. At Portland we had to wait an hour for the tug "Forest Queen" which took us out two miles where "Vancouver" was anchored. The water being low, she could not come in to dock.

Several people came to see the Macy's off, even to the 'Vancouver', indeed almost everyone had friends to see them on board so the tug had quite a number to bring back. It rained off and on all day and at six it settled down to heavy rain continuing all night- with a heavy fog and quite a swell sending many down below. At two we had lunch. I felt so poorly that I just took a cup of tea and a bun. After four when we had passed all places of interest such as Cushen Island, Cousin Island, Peak Island, and Cape Elizabeth, I went below and took off my dress, slept for two hours, when my head was so much better, up and dressed and ate a good dinner at six.

Captain Macy had me put between him and Sally at the

Captain's table so I am well looked after. For dinner, I had soup, Pigeon pie, Rice Pudding, nuts and raisins, just the thing for seasickness, but I am as steady as a rock. Poor Mrs. Macy went to bed ill at four and Ella left her dinner after ordering it. Captain Macy introduced me to the ship's captain, and a gentleman who is one of the head owners of the Dominion Line, as a niece of Lord Aylmer, who crossed on the last voyage. Old Dick, (the steward who Mrs G. was telling Auntie about,) came and spoke to me as Miss Woodburn, but alas he is not on my side of the ship. But I think my steward is nice and ours is the nicest stewardess on board. She has been kind to me.

I had a lovely bath, seawater, at eight, but after this I am to have it at seven; the steward calls me, and gets the water ready. The great chill off, I had a soak before breakfast. Now about the Passengers- there are a great many already and as many more will join at Halifax. A party of thirteen men and women, are on board with Bicycles, who are to wheel around England. There are five children, all seem nice; I have not spoken to anyone, so cannot say how nice they really are.

"Vancouver's" cabins are quite large and the Stewardess thinks I have mine alone. I hope so as there is little room for two. I am quite close to the bathroom etc. and in a quite warm part of the ship. It is very cold where the Macy's are, and the Saloons are cold.

I went to bed at eight o'clock and slept well. At seven this morning the fog horn awoke me and, thinking grandmother was calling me, for I was dreaming about her, I sat up hitting my head a great crack, which brought me to my senses. I then had to get out (and that is hard work) and bathe my forehead with cold water as I was afraid of a black eye. However, I only have a swelled one - which I hope is not very noticeable.

The attention is very good. There are a number of men in the dining room, and twelve tables, the longest of which the Captain and Chief Officers fill, with a few at a third. I had a time hunting for my cabin box. It had been put in with the Macy's by mistake, and three stewards were hunting for it for near an hour in everyone's cabin, and just as I began to fear it was in the Hold, it was found.

How stupid it was of me to forget that I could not post a Canadian card in the States after addressing three at home. However, Mr. Earnest Macy got me two at Portland, so I wrote one to you standing against the wall and I will now send one to Melbourne, as I thought, dear Mother, you would like a letter. When you write be sure and say how Lord Aylmer is. And be sure to tell how your wrist feels. I do hope you will not try and do too much. You must get the boys to help you well.

Some of the people have lovely flowers. The room I am in is sweet with great bowls of roses etc. Captain Macy got a bunch of sweet flowers at Portland and I keep them in my room. While they keep fresh, I will wear them at dinner. There are two old ladies talking near me, and one has just told the other that nineteen years ago, she was operated on for appendicitis, and since then she has been much stronger. This is the third time she has crossed and she has been on all our Canadian Great Lakes.

It is getting brighter so I hope the fog will lift so we can see about us. The Table Steward (ours) has just come up and told Sally and me that the ship will get in to Halifax at half past three or four, and will remain in dock all night, so we can go on land. So Sally and I are going to see a bit of the city. I will wait to finish this tonight. There is a child talking to me so it is hard to write.

Stopover in Halifax

Saturday morning 9 o'clock—

S.S. Vancouver did not arrive at Halifax till four last night; fog prevented our making good time. She lay off a little distance to take on coal from a barge, which continued all night; fortunately, the coal hole was not on my side of the ship. I remained on deck until eleven, just going down for supper, had tea with Mr. Lawrence, who is the head of the Dominion Line. He asked us for an oyster supper, alas I could not, so had bread and jam. Just after dinner three of us sang College songs. A 'Lady English' from British Columbia who has lived there eight years, is going home with husband and children. She has a beautiful deep voice and is very jolly and there was a young woman who composes on the piano very well. I hope we will have more musical people on later.

Two Bishops are to come on board here and forty more people; a few just came in now. We have finished breakfast and in a few minutes we are to go on shore. Before breakfast we crossed the deck a little way to see a ship-load of Polish Jews, who have just arrived a few hours later than us. They are very different looking people. All wore top boots, men had hats, women bright little shawls tied on under their chins and many wore fur coats with the skin outside and some were beautifully embroidered. They look good-natured and are on their way to Manitoba.

I must close as we are to go on shore. I will post this and a C.P.S. to Edward. There have been three mails on board. I wonder if I will get a letter from Liverpool. Mrs. Macy and the girls send you their love and say to tell you how pleased they are to have my company. Mrs. Macy and Ella are alright today as we were anchored for the night; people on the side of the vessel near the coal holes got little sleep though.

There are many rich people here but I am as well dressed as most, and Sally and Ella look their best - dresses fit well. The food is first-class. We have beautiful fruit - all kinds, even strawberries and cream. Although game is out of season we are well fed and ought to get fat. The sea salt water bath is grand, but I have not lost my cold yet. I feel as if we had been at sea a week, and it seems ages since I left home.

Love to the McKenzies, with much to you all from your loving daughter & sister

Emmie Woodburn

Emmie Nearly Misses the Boat

S.S. Vancouver

Sunday May 2nd 1897

My Darling Mother,

We are out of sight of land and quite a fog is on us. A vessel that came in to Halifax while we were in dock found the fog thick off the Labrador Coast. Many are seasick this morning, the stewardess said, although there is little swell on. Old Dick has just done talking to me. He is so nice, very friendly to me, talks to me every time he sees me.

How I wish the "Vancouver" had not taken on passengers at

Halifax. For alas, I have a lady in my room, about forty years of age, who is dreadfully ill with a cold so coughed all night. The lady next to me has a difficult baby who cried most of the night, so I had a poor night's rest. Dick says if things are not better tonight, he will have things changed.

Two such, indeed I may say three, such pretty girls came on board yesterday. One has a brother who looks nice and is very polite. Captain, Mrs., and the Miss Macys came on land at eleven yesterday. We first went to a friend of the Captain who lives in a big meeting room and sells books; he gave me a bunch of tracts. There we had lunch and Mrs. Macy remained while we went off to see the city.

I took the lead and made for the citadel. There we were challenged by the Sentinel. I said we were off the S.S.Vancouver and wanted to view the city from the citadel wall which is on a hill and very high. He said we might, so we crossed the moat over a drawbridge and had to sign our names, after which a guide (an Irish soldier with a mighty brogue) took us about to see the view of that city and for miles and miles about. And the harbour, one of the largest in the world, was grand in places. The forest was very thick. The walk on top of the fort was near a mile long and at every few yards a cannon was placed. On both sides of the harbour are cannons placed in the woods for defence. Of course I had to tip the man, but it was worth a quarter to see the view, and it was the only way we could have any idea of the size.

Then we all went to see the best streets and to do some shopping for Sally. Captain and Mrs. Macy and their friend Mr. Lyman went off to see some good Christians. Well the ship was to sail at half past three and we waited a long way up town till twenty minutes past and were not called for. I decided we must leave a message at the store where they were to call for us and then make a dash for the ship.

We arrived and found 'Vancouver' almost ready to start. Visiting friends were leaving the vessel. We were in an awful fright and Ella talked our head off. I longed to shake her, however, in a little the travelers arrived, hot and tired. They did not come until almost four, but the ship was late in starting at half past four when she began to leave her dock. And it took an hour to turn her and shove clear of the Pier. At last we were off. Until dinner time the view going out of harbour was lovely. After dinner we sat on deck until nine. I had hot lemonade and a biscuit and went off to bed.

A Wicked Woman Fears Death

Sunday

With the Bishops we are sure to have a fine service this morning. I hope it will be by Bishop Courtany this morning as I have heard him. He is very eloquent. They are going over to join the other Bishops from all over the world for the Queen's Jubilee. Bishops are to line the steps of St. Paul's Cathedral in robes of office when the Queen goes up.

Sunday evening

There was a short service at eleven. Bishop Courtany preached a fine sermon, but very few came in for it. There was a collection for widows and orphans of sailors. In the afternoon I read and later played Hymns. This evening a service was held in the Saloon. I went to bed at nine as I was tired and disappointed not to have got a letter from home.

Monday 3rd May

I slept last night in a hurry as my hip bothered me. I think I walked too much so this morning I have been very quiet. There is a very rich lady, handsome, with a lame husband and a child. The child, a beautiful boy of three is so sweet. She has spent most of her life travelling and now they are going to England, Ireland, Scotland and the continent for five years. I like to talk to her. She is so bright. She told me today that my steward had told her I was the daughter of an Earl so I set her straight on that account.

This morning a party, Sally and I among them, went below to see the horses. There are ninety-one on board, some of them handsome, others poor creatures. Their stalls are so small they cannot move or lie down and are not cleaned, even the stall. One of the horses is huge- nineteen and a half hands high. There are twelve hundred barrels of Canadian apples on board and a great pile of railway rails that are worn out and are going over to England to be melted and used for the same purpose again. There is no place in America where this can be done.

A Mrs.Gordon who sings and plays very well, is very like Mrs. Jack Aylmer, the same way of speaking and talkative. She has two children, a boy of seven and a sweet little girl of two, who amuses everyone. Mrs. Macy and Ella are quite well now. Sally is very nice. I like her.

We are dreadfully over-crowded in this cabin. I do not like being cooped up with Mrs. Worsely who is ill and stays in her berth. I broke the crystal of my watch trying to get out of bed and dropped my comb, breaking half the teeth today. I am glad that I did not take your new comb as I would have felt worse if it had gone. I suppose I should be grateful for Cousin Tom's generosity, but all the same, I do wish for a private cabin.

We had music for some time last night. Mrs. Gordon sang, Mrs. Le Port French played and sang with their husbands, and Mr. McDonald sang and played. The Le Port French's are from Vancouver (also the Gordons). They are rich and she is very pretty. He can drink a pint of beer for lunch, a pint of wine for dinner, and a glass of brandy for supper. She is worse. The Bishops are very jolly. They keep their table laughing. Bishop Courtany has three pair of twins. Bishop Kingdon is small and not so nice.

Last night the fog was so thick that we had to stand still. The Captain thinks we will not get in to Liverpool until tomorrow week. At five this morning we passed a large Iceberg, or rather it passed us along with an open boat. Two men called out that they had 'plenty fish'. The weather is dreadfully cold. I hope it will be warmer tomorrow as we will be well away from the banks.

There is a nice looking English lady of about sixty, from Chicago, sitting near me. She says I am so like a friend of hers (about my age) who died a few months ago, that she likes to watch me. This is the first time she has spoken, but ever since I came on board she has been wanting to talk to me. Everyone is very kind to me but I will be glad when I get into a good bed again in my own room.

As you know the cream we get on porridge, pudding, and fruit is the Cleeve Condensed Cream thinned with milk or water. The milk is also condensed. We get such beautiful strawberries, pineapples, and all kinds of fruit, also ice cream. Their bread is so good, also pastry for breakfast. We get beautiful hot cakes and pancakes with maple syrup. I eat three meals but don't manage any more. (You will be glad to hear dear mother that all the pimples have left my face.)

I have been wondering all day how you are dear Mother. I do so worry about your health. Did you all go to church yesterday and did you think of me? I wonder if the choir sang the hymns for those at sea. Mr. Hepburn said they would for me.

Wednesday May 5th

My face is badly burnt today and looks quite fat. Last night about dinner time the temperature changed so very much that we were nearly choked with heat. I never was hotter than last night. I lay with only a sheet over me and today we are out without jackets. This is wonderful but we are in the Gulf Stream and the water is only sixty-six degrees. There is a big swell on. Last night at supper the ship began to toss and turn. In spite of the frantic rush of stewards, plates and glass were flying about, many being smashed to pieces.

I had an awful night with my room companion, Mrs. Worsely. She screamed and cried with fright and walked about calling for help. The Stewards were running in and out. Finally she said to the Steward she knew we were being drowned. I'd had just about enough and said, "Well you must be a wicked woman to be so afraid to die!"

As soon as I was dressed I told the Steward he must move me. I could not stand another night like the last, so the lady who thinks I am so like her friend is going to take me in. Two others have also kindly offered to share their room. Another reason I must leave Mrs. Worsely is she will not bathe.

The ship is rolling very much but Sally and I think it fine. The Captain is nice. He talked to me for a long time today calling me Miss Macy. He says we will be half way over tonight. We went three hundred miles out of our way to the South to avoid ice which will delay us a day. Sally and I have walked and sat out all day enjoying the toss. Many are ill below. All day there have been 'three of Mother Carrey's chicks' following us. They are a sort of seabird that come before storms but the sailors say we will have a fine voyage all the same. This is the first day since I left home (a week tonight) that we were to see the sun. At noon we passed, or rather there crossed our bows a large sailing vessel, likely bound for Quebec. They did not signal but the Captain thinks she is Danish.

Mrs. Deveroux Observes a Family Resemblance in Emmie

The young lady traveling with the Macys bears such an uncanny resemblance to the late daughter of my dear friend, Lucy French, that I cannot take my eyes off her. It is terribly unsettling to feel I have met up with a ghost. For, indeed, Miss Woodburn and Miss French could have been twin sisters. I don't know that the French family will ever get over the loss of their dear girl. Who could? She was such a lovely young woman. The Lord works in strange ways! I will never understand why the young with so much to offer are taken and those who are old and afflicted are left on earth to suffer.

I feel uneasy about Miss Woodburn. There's just something not right there that sends chills up my spine. She doesn't look well but I cannot quite put my finger on what it is. Perhaps I am just an old woman with far too many morbid thoughts. I must put them out of my mind. Still, I have an inclination to look after her and see that she is safe. The poor girl is having such an awful time with that dreadful Mrs. Worsely! I shall invite Miss Woodburn to move in to my cabin at once. At least she will get some peace and quiet and a decent sleep at night. I can't have her arriving in Ireland exhausted from the journey.

Perhaps there is a connection to my friends, the French's. She tells me her Grandmother who died last year was Louisa French, the daughter of a British officer who had been stationed in India. He married a fourteen-year-old girl, the daughter of a Portuguese army officer, who eventually had twenty-two children. God forbid! Mind you, more than half of the infants died. Conditions are so primitive in the East Indies that the babies just don't survive. That French family came out to Canada in 1823 and were given a large land grant in the Eastern Townships in exchange for the army pension.

Miss Woodburn lives with her family on this land still. She has such an adventurous spirit. It's odd that such a handsome young woman is not married yet. She is indeed accomplished. She sings and plays piano and speaks so well. Why she even graduated from College! Surely she is quite the catch! There is a young doctor on board who would be a fine match for her. I must speak to Mrs. Chapman, for she is well acquainted with him, and arrange a meeting with Miss Woodburn. You never know what might come of it. I am not too old to play at the game of matchmaking and it makes me feel young to be around the young folk.

Perhaps Miss Woodburn would consider being my travelling companion on my trip across the Continent. Even though it is wonderful to be able to travel, I am lonely. She would be marvellous company and it would do her good to exercise that clever mind of hers. How I think she would blossom to see places like the Louvre, Venice or the Vatican! Yes, I am resolved to ask her to come with me. I have such an unexplained desire to look after that girl.

The Voyage Comes to an End

Thursday May 6.

The sailors are painting many parts of the ship. Every two weeks - twice a month - the vessel is painted so that sailors are at this work most of the time. I am moved in with Mrs. Deveroux. She is very nice and I slept well last night. A lady, Mrs. Chapman from Montreal, came up to me last night and asked me if I would allow her to introduce a young man to me who is most anxious to know me. She says he is of a good genteel family and very nice. I gave her leave so she asked my name, however the young man has not turned up yet, so I do not know what he is like.

The Captain had a long walk and talk with me today. He is very nice. This day next week most of us will be at our destination. I hear we are to have a concert Saturday night and a sacred one on Sunday. This will be a change. It is becoming very monotonous on board, people will not play games, dance or sing. Ella is too lazy to walk so I see little of her. Sally and I are great friends.

Friday May 7.

Last night Mrs. Chapman brought the young man who was so anxious to know me up and I walked with him for an hour. He is studying to be a doctor, is nice, but quite a boy. You know, dear mother, boys always fancy girls older than themselves.

This morning I had such a nice long talk with Mrs. Deveroux. She is very sweet and kind and, do you know, she knows of many we know. She is very well connected and has traveled nearly all over the world. You must not tell this. One of her daughters was engaged to our cousin Camfield Faloon but he jilted her. She is now married to someone else. The Deveroux lived in Toronto for three years and were great friends of the Winders and know the Brents and Mrs. Laurier, and Mrs. D. knows the Butlers of Kilkenny, cousins of our Miss Butlers and when she was a girl she met Mr. Gerald Aylmer. She is related to titled people. The girl I so resemble was a daughter of a Miss French. I wonder if there can be any connection?

This morning Old Dick, the steward, took us to see the Kitchens and Engine Room. It is wet this afternoon and as I am rather under the weather, I will not go on deck again tonight. Last night we had some nice music.

Saturday 8th.

This has been the nicest day out. The water is so blue and the sun bright, so bright that my face is like fire. We have had a fine voyage, no storms. So if all goes well tomorrow (four o'clock) we will be in sight of old Ireland. Three passengers are to get off there. Today there were so many beautiful seagulls following us.

Monday 10th.

Monday morning, great excitement! We are once more near land. At twenty minutes to eight last night we saw land and at eight the first lighthouse. At two this morning we reached Moville. Three passengers got off at half past three. Then we were off again and from there we have had such a lovely view of land. The grass looks so very green from the distance. The first officer is very nice and lent me his glass so I could see the train going into Belfast. There were a good many vessels in sight. Early yesterday one ran quite close to us from Glasgow to Belfast and a few minutes ago we saw a shipwreck. Only the masts were to be seen. The officer said she was driven onto the rocks nearly a year ago in a thick fog.

Everyone is very happy this morning, it is so smooth. Yesterday there was a great swell on. I could not write yesterday as I had a very bad headache and spent most of the day in bed. Finally I went to the Doctor and he gave me some salts and a sleeping powder. He said I looked ill and so I did, although was burnt still. My eyes were dreadfully swelled.

I was so very lonely I could have cried. However, I felt better by evening and had supper. I could not eat much at dinner. Saturday I could not hear the concert as my head got so bad by eight I went to bed. Today I am quite well again, I am glad to say. We have had a very fine trip, no storm, and yesterday was the first day we had a bad swell - and it was bad. Such a lot of dishes were broken. I sat on deck with Mr. Douglas, my young friend, until eleven but did not stay up to see the rudder come off. Mr. D. said that the tugboats steer the ship into dock and do not want interference from the rudder.

It has begun to rain, I hate to say. If cousin Dawse does not meet me, the Captain will let me stay on board tonight and I will go over to Holyhead in the morning. I am so anxious to arrive in Old Ireland at last.

There are a few on board to whom I will be very sorry to say good-bye. They have been so very kind to me, especially Mrs. Deveroux. Mrs. Chapman offered to take me with her as her guest to Paris, but of course I should not accept so much from a stranger. I have written to Ethel by this mail. Please read the boys this letter that I am enclosing. I will send a post card when I arrive in Limerick and write next week.

I hope the Insurance is settled. Every day I wonder what father has decided to do. I will be very anxious until I hear. Mrs. Macy and the girls send you their love. They have been very kind to me. Tell Dr. McKenzie there is a young doctor on board who is very nice and we have many a quarrel. I am keeping my head in all. I have him to fight with; he, the doctor, is twenty-two and just through school and now on his way to the Edinburgh Hospitals, then to London. The Doctor on board is also nice; he is going to take me to see the surgery in an hour.

And now dear parents, I will stop this long letter and when I post, will write on the envelope if Cousin Cleeve meets me. We will pass the Island of Mann at twelve, reaching Liverpool at six.

With much love to you all. Ever dear Father, Mother, Harry & Ben.

Your loving daughter and sister,
        Emmie Woodburn

~~~~~

THREE

Emmie Arrives In Ireland

Cousin Dawse Frets Over Missing Emmie

Well here's a fine how-de-do! I've just met up with my man Rodgers, and he tells me that I've missed Cousin Emmie. It seems she refused to allow him to take her to a hotel to get a room for the night. He met her at the ship right enough but Emmie insisted on going on ahead to Dublin on the overnight steamer. Rodgers has just delivered Emmie, baggage and all, to the ferry dock. It seems I'm too late to intercept her.

Whatever is the girl thinking? She'll arrive in Ireland exhausted after her long trans-Atlantic crossing. If she'd only waited an hour for me, I'd have taken care of everything. Emmie must be an awfully forward sort of girl to venture out on her own, especially at night. Now I'm in hot water for not looking after her properly. Uncle Ben will definitely disapprove of this mess.

Well, I'll just have to make the best of it. It's not my fault the girl is headstrong. I'll have to wire Uncle Ben and give him the heads up to collect her at the ferry docks in the morning. That is such a rough location and I wouldn't want Emmie getting mixed up in THAT crowd all on her own! There's no telling what harm she might come to.

So I'd better make haste to the telegraph office. Now what ever am I going to say? Guess I'd better just stick to the facts:

TELEGRAM TO:

>MR. BEN JOURNEAUX ESQ.
>15 PALMERSTON ROAD
>RATHMINES DUBLIN

EMMIE ARRIVED SAFELY STOP
HAS TAKEN OVERNIGHT STEAMER STOP
ARRIVES DUBLIN 6 AM STOP
SEND CARRIAGE STOP
DAWSE CLEEVE FULL STOP

Well that ought to do it. Now that I don't have to take Emmie to dinner, I could get back to the office and finish those last orders that came in today. Yes, business couldn't be better. The orders for butter and cream are coming in hand over fist for the Jubilee. Good old Queen Victoria! She can have as many public celebrations as she pleases with my blessing. Cleeve Brothers will be rolling in profits at the end of the day.

Emmie Sends a Post Card to Her Family at Home

15 Palmerston Road, Dublin

Tuesday 11th May

Darling Mother.

This is a quick note to let you know I have arrived at Uncle Ben's. Cousin Dawse could not meet me and Frank was in London, so they sent a young man to meet me. He said I could go to an hotel for the night and then on to Dublin today. But I thought it best to come direct, to book a steamer from the dock an hour after the 'Vancouver' got in. Cousin Dawse telegraphed to Uncle that I had left so they were up when I got in at seven.

How I enjoyed the drive this morning, but am tired as I've had a bad night crossing. I did not sleep much. I was shocked to see that Uncle Ben is much changed and his memory is gone. Aunt Mary said not to mind anything he wrote as he does not remember much —makes things up to his fancy.

I had no chance to post this in Liverpool as I did not leave the dock and had no stamps. The Tom Cleeves are in London so I will stay here with Ben and Mary Journeaux till I hear from them. I will write in a day or two. Good bye darlings.

Emmie

Emmie's First Days in Dublin

15 Palmerston Road

May 14th 1897

My Darling Mother,

Since I arrived, I have had nine letters welcoming me to Ireland. Cousin Ruth is not well and is at the seaside in Wales, so that is why she did not come to meet me with Cousin Dawse. He has asked me to make him a long visit to London and Miss Cornelle has asked me there as well.

This morning, Friday, Aunt Mary had a letter from Phoebe Cleeve. She and Tom are coming from England tonight and will arrive at five o'clock. Tomorrow morning Cousin Tom will go on to Limerick and Phoebe will stay here for a few days. I can either go down to Limerick with her or remain on in Dublin longer, just as I wish. Aunt Morris wants me to pay her a visit when I can.

Indeed I cannot tell how kind everyone is to me. If only all at home was O.K. I should be very happy. Aunt had Canada letters from Ethel and Mrs. Aylmer yesterday. I was so thankful to hear from Ethel that Edward had got work. I hope it is good and pays well. And father, what is he to do? I had hoped to get a letter from him before this.

Now I will tell you everything since the 'Vancouver' reached dock. I had so many new friends to say good-bye to. Mrs. Chapman wanted me so much to go up to London as her guest for a few weeks and then to Paris. But of course, I would not. She has given me her London address and if I am ever there, I will go and see her. Young Dr. Douglas professed to be very sorry to say good-bye and said if he could hear I was in London, he would go down from Edinburgh to see me. But I shall take care that he will not know if I ever go to London, poor boy!

When the vessel stopped I was very disappointed not to see anyone I knew, however, Mr. Rodgers found me and was very nice. As I told you, I did not like to go to an hotel with a stranger in case Cousin Dawse was not there. However, since then I have had a letter from Dawse and he said he was so sorry not to have seen me. He was at the hotel by eight o'clock.

The Vancouver got in at half past six. By the time I collected my trunks and was through the Customs it was half past seven and the direct boat for Dublin (nearby) left at eight so I had not long to wait. But, oh it was cold! I was half frozen before I went to bed and the night was awful, so rough I thought we would have been drowned. I hardly slept a wink although the bed was better than those on the "Vancouver".

After six, we got into Dublin. As I thought I would go to Limerick yesterday, I left the trunks at the dock. At a few minutes after seven, I was in Uncle Ben and Aunt Mary's arms. Cousin Phil Wright was with them too and it was he who met me at the docks. He works in Dublin. He is very nice and handsome. Aunt looks well, but Uncle is so old, very bent, and his memory is very bad. He is very cross, at times cannot bear a noise, yet is quite deaf. Aunt Mary's dog, Floss, remembered me.

I caught such a cold in Liverpool that I find it hard to make Uncle Ben hear me. My voice is very weak and I had only just got over a cold while at sea. After breakfast, Aunt Mary and I went to Aunt Morris and the Tyndalls. They did not expect me so were greatly surprised. That afternoon we went over to visit the Lodges and there, the Bradleys and Aunt Morris, and several other cousins came in. So by night I had seen seventeen old friends!

Wednesday, in the morning, Uncle Ben and I went for a walk and I got a pair of shoes that cost three dollars. In the afternoon, Uncle took me to hear a celebrated band from Austria. The Lodges were here for tea. Evelyn is so cramped that she has lost her beauty. They will be going on the Continent for a month, but are giving me a party on Monday.

Yesterday, Aunt Mary thought, as my black dress was so long, and this is such a dusty world, I had better get a short walking dress ready made that would do all the year round. So, as she is not able to go into town, Adam Tyndall and I went off shopping. I got a lovely suit of shepherd's plaid, which I paid eleven dollars for. It fits like a glove. (I also got you a lace mourning veil which I enclose.)

We had lunch in town after we were through. I took a cab and got my trunks up from the docks. Alan and Ada had arrived for tea. As it was Aunt Mary's birthday, we had some visitors, among them, Mrs. Davis, Jennie Cleeve's cousin, and a friend of Miss Gordon's. Cousin Phil Wright comes here nearly every night. Aunt says Mrs. Wright will ask me there for a visit.

Aunt Morris is a wonder! She is so bright. Mrs. Lodge wants to see me too, so I will go around there today. Aunt Mary wants me to live with her. Do you remember when I was here before she took a fancy to me? If she likes me so much, I wish she would remember me in her will, but she will leave all to Aunt Morris, and Aunt Morris all to her, and both to Cousin Evelyn. Evelyn and her mother are very rich indeed!

I must stop now. I will not write again until the end of next week. Kiss dear Father and the boys for me. Ever darling Mother.

Your loving child,

Emmie

Emmie Writes to Her Younger Brothers

15 Palmerston Road

May 16

My Dear Harry and Ben,

I was so glad to get the home letters last night. They were sent up from Limerick even though all the Tom Cleeves were away from home. Cousin Phoebe came this morning, but Cousin Tom had to go direct to Limerick as Saturday is farmer's day. Phoebe and I are to go down on Wednesday.

This morning we all went out for a walk. Phoebe sent for cousin Cecil who is at a school out of town and he came and spent Sunday here. He rode up on his bike about one o'clock. He is not good looking at all and is very bold. He had been off all morning on the tram car spending money.

I met Mrs. J. Wright in the street. She did not know me but I stopped her. She thinks I have changed and grown tall but everyone tells me that. Alice came up for tea later and we played cards. Now it is bedtime, only I am not sleepy. Aunt Morris comes in every day. I cannot make her or Uncle hear me, my voice is so low and they are very deaf. I do wish this cold would leave me.

The country is looking beautiful. I wish you could see the greens, horse chestnuts, and Laburnum. Also the lilies are in blossom, so the air is sweet with delightful smells.

Monday 17th

Yesterday we were a big party for dinner. Mr. and Mrs. Gibson generally come here Sunday and Phil brought two Cleeves making eight in all. I was so glad to see the Gibsons. Miss G. is looking thin and old but we had a nice long talk.

After our visitors left, Phil and I went off for a long walk, which was lovely, along the banks of the Don. At one place where I crossed, the stepping stones were very slippery. I had to get Phil to help me as I did not want to take a bath with my new dress and shoes. We walked so far that, of course, we were late for tea, even though we hurried at the last.

After tea, Uncle Ben, Phil, and I went to church. (In the morning, we all went.) It was a happy day and no time to feel homesick as I was petted and made so much of. I often thought of you all. Do you know there has not been one drop of rain since I came to Old Ireland, a week tonight. Is not that a grand welcome?

Young Cecil Cleeve has attached himself to me. He says he is very fond of me and climbs on my knee and hugs and kisses me. But I am not fond of him! He is bold and talks in a very nasty way. He says he wants me to marry some Limerick man so that I can live in Ireland and then he will stay with me. Cheeky boy! I long to give him a good solid blow.

May 18

We have just come in from town. I find Rathmines very much built up with streets full of new houses, some very nice. Uncle Ben's garden is beautiful, gay with bright flowers and the green house is sweet with lovely roses. Cousin Phoebe has been shopping and I was with her but I did not get anything except for stamps.

We all went over to the Lodges last night and had a very nice evening, with a grand tea- like a dinner, two maids to wait on us. Mrs. Cleeve wore black satin, Aunt silk, and I wore my black velvet skirt and silk waist. Everyone was so good to me. I am petted and made much of because I look thin and as the tan is worn off, am pale.

Aunt said today that if I spent the summer in Limerick, she and Aunt Morris would like me to stay for the winter. But I think I will go home for Christmas. I had another letter from Miss Cornelle urging me to go to Bristol now by boat from Dublin, which is a lovely run. But I have written to say I cannot come this summer. If I go to England, it must be after I leave Ireland on account of the expense.

Tell mother my new dress is much admired and is so comfortable. The jacket is lined with silk. Mrs.Cleeve has just got three new dresses. They cost thirty-five, forty, and fifty-five dollars; a lot of money to spend on clothes!

I will close now and will write to mother when I see Limerick. We go tomorrow. Be good to mother. Ever dear Harry and Ben,

Your loving sister,

Emmie.

On to Limerick and Sunville House

Sunville House

Saturday 22nd May

My Dear Father and Mother,

We missed our train on Wednesday, so spent a lovely afternoon at the Sea. The salt breeze did us good. My cold is much better. Thursday we took the early train to Limerick. Cousin Tom and the Governess (she left yesterday) met us after dinner. Joe telephoned over to say that Cousin Kathleen, Miss Perret, and the children were coming over to see me.

Cousin Kathleen is very sweet and welcomed me most warmly. The children were shy. Cousin Mary also came in on a Bike on her way to town. After she left, I went over to see Aunt Sophia and remained until six. In the evening, Cousin Tom took me to Beechlawn to see Cousin Joe and then on to Fernbank, Fred's home. His wife, Jennie, is very delicate; some inward trouble from what I hear, much like you dear mother. Their daughter, Olive is very tall. She has just earned a musical diploma.

Dear mother, they all received me so warmly and I am told to go to any house whenever I wish. I am sure I will grow young and fat with all the petting. Yesterday I spent the morning with Aunt Sophia. She is little changed and so worldly. She and Lord Aylmer did not get on very well, though she is very fond of Fred Aylmer.

We had dinner at three, a horrid hour, with Mrs. Tom Cleeve and Mrs. Thompson. She was Miss Kirkham, the governess here for years. She is now visiting and is not very strong. Her home is in Cork and in a short time she must return. I like her very much.

I went over to Beechlawn as it was Kathleen's day to entertain. She is such a sweet little hostess and her sister is so nice too. Cousin Mary and Jack came in and I met two other old friends. We sat in a lovely big room. It's a new one, for Billiards as well as for sitting. Mrs. Cleeve called for Tom to join us later at Beechlawn. All the Cleeves go there for Friday night so we made quite a number.

Mrs. Tom Cleeve is a good woman. We have family prayers every day, also grace. She is very nice to me. At present she has the house turned upside down. Three rooms are to be papered and nearly all the carpets and curtains over the house are up. All the same, the house is very nice, though much too big.

There is a lovely green house here, and the gardens will soon be lovely with roses. This is such a big house, fourteen bedrooms and lots of sitting rooms. I do not know where to find people when I want them. I feel quite lost but have a nice room opposite a beautiful bathroom where I take a bath every morning.

There are three maids here; cook, housemaid, and parlour maid and that is not enough for so big a house. There ought to be a housekeeper. I was nearly two hours at the flowers today! Then head and tailed gooseberries for a pie while Mrs. Tom made the paste. She is hard at work all mornings with sleeves rolled up and a big apron on.

All the Cleeve brothers work hard, particularly Joe and Fred. Fred gets up at five or six every morning and goes to work before breakfast - the same with Joe. They say Joe is the one to do the planning - he is very clever. Tom is traveling much of the time and is hardly ever here for dinner. Sometimes he is not home till nine or ten at night, after having nothing to eat since breakfast.

The Cleeve brothers are very busy now as the Jubilee gives them larger orders for London. There is much less fresh milk consumed in big cities, now the Cleeves are so well known. (We had nothing else for our tea and fruit on board ship coming over.) It is expected that two millions of people will visit London next month for the festivities.

The view of the Shannon from these front windows is lovely. We see all the ships and boats coming into Limerick. Wish I could sketch some of them but they pass by too quickly. The day I arrived, a big cargo of sugar from the south of France came in. The Cleeves get a cargo every month.

I am to go over to Cousin Mary's today after dinner and learn to ride. They are all determined I shall ride a bike. I do not care much to learn only everyone says I must. There are very few in Limerick who do not ride. I am using Cousin Eileen's wheel and hope I will not break my head!

I also have some sewing to do. Mary says I must make my own cotton waists as they are very expensive to buy. She will fit me. I quite forgot the frill for my velvet dress so will have to make a new one.

The gong has just rung for dinner so I must go. We have breakfast at half past eight, dinner at three and tea at seven - nasty hours, but they suit Cousin Tom. I do hope, dear Mother, that you will not try to do too much. Give my love to all.

With lots of kisses ever dear parents.

Your loving child,

Emmie Woodburn

Life Amongst the Wealthy

Sunville House

May 24th 1897

My Dear Father,

This is the 24th. In an hour you will be up and hard at work, while I am lazy and have no cares or work. Indeed it is very strange how I have settled down to do nothing. As my hip has been bothering me, I cannot even do fancy work. But I hope next week to be more energetic and do some painting and good reading etc. I have promised Cousin Mary to make her some wine glass doilies, so I must set to work. Mrs. Tom is very busy in the morning, but in the afternoon she goes out, and in the evening does nothing. None of the ladies here do much sewing of any kind. Even Cousin Mary says she has got lazy.

I sent my last letter on Saturday. That day was spent at Bracken Brae where I tried the Bike, but I tired very soon. It will take a lot of practice. In the evening, Ted Cleeve came down from the creamery at Mallow where he is living for now and spent the evening here. Yesterday, all the Cleeves plus Mr. & Mrs. Thompson, (Mr. Thompson comes to spend Sunday with his wife) went to church at the Cathedral. Cousin Mary, Joe and Kathleen Cleeve were also there.

After a five-course dinner at Sunville, we all went under the trees till five when Joe came over and brought me to Beechlawn for tea. Mary and Aunt Sophia were there. After tea we all went over to Bracken Brae except for Fred's wife, Jennie, who is so delicate that she does not join the family parties.

All day yesterday I thought of my family and wondered what you all would be doing. I always wonder how the garden is coming along. They pet me so much here that I am not homesick, though sometimes I am lonely for my parents. Tom is very good to me and pets me like a Father.

Aunt Sophia is so kind and gave me a lovely silk parasol. She had a few sent out from town for me to choose from. I took a lovely hunter's green, as the most serviceable and it could go with any dress. Aunt says I must not get too much sun. She worries about my hip though it is nearly well. I only feel it if I walk a great deal.

Mary said to come for lunch and then we can go over to

Fernbank for afternoon tea. People here are always eating and they laugh at me when I say no thanks, as I am afraid I will be ill from too much food. We had five kinds of fresh vegetable for dinner yesterday. They were delicious. (I only took three kinds.).

Fernbank, Fred's home, has the most land and lovely gardens, all kinds of fruit and vegetables, nice flowers, beautiful stables, summer house and tent. The house, Mary says, is the best placed, not pretty on the outside, but they will do it up and build a veranda next year which will improve it.

Beechlawn has the finest trees, and I almost think the prettiest grounds. Sunville House is the grandest and best-laid-out, Bracken Brae the cosiest. There is a lot of land there too, but the house is not well placed and the rooms are small.

May 28

Tuesdays, Cousin Phoebe always stays in, and when the weather is fine, there is tea in the garden. But as it was wet, we had tea in the house today. I made a nice cake. A few ladies called in the morning along with Olive and Miss Haddlsey. (Olive is the oldest child I ever met. Her manner is so self-possessed and she is very quiet.) In the evening, Joe, Kathleen and Fred came over. Wednesday we walked into town but drove home on a sidecar, as my hip was tired. I had to hold on going around the curves.

Yesterday was Ascension Day, so Dick the coachman drove us in to the Cathedral on the sidecar. I enjoyed the ride very much as it did not shake today - had not to hold on at all. Cousin Phoebe and I remained for Holy Communion. After Church, I got gloves for Mother, and two pretty flowers for myself. We walked home during the factory dinner hour and got mixed up with about 150 working women and girls. This was not nice at all! I should hate to have to work in a smelly factory in the heat with such a great crowd of people.

Later, we drove out to the Fogarty's for tennis. They live at Westburn, Uncle Ben's old home. It is a lovely place well back from the road, but perhaps you remember it, dear father. The Fogartys were kind to me and gave me a nice Irish welcome. I did not play tennis as my hip was tired from two days walking back from town. As long as it bothers me, I will not play.

I do try not to fret or think sad things, as I want to get strong. Cousin Phoebe will not let me do any sewing until I have had a good rest. She says time enough. This is Beechlawn's day to receive callers so we will go for afternoon tea and stay till eleven. Too bad Mrs. Thompson is going home today. I will miss her very much.

How I wish you were here, Father. It would be so nice to go over the different places of interest together. When my hip is well, I will go to visit Grandfather's and Grandmother's graves at St. John's Church. Yesterday after church at St. Mary's, I went to visit dear cousin Janie Aylmer's grave. The stone is plain white, very nice and it is in a pretty spot under a copper Beech tree.

But enough of sad things. Tell mother I must send her gloves on their own, as they are too heavy. I will write to the boys in the morning. Kiss the little mother for me.

Your loving child,

Emmie Woodburn

Phoebe Cleeve Writes to Emmie's Mother

Sunville House

25th May 1897

My Dearest Bel,

Indeed I cannot say when I have met such a fine young woman as your dear daughter, Emmie. You and Willie have done a capital job of raising her. She has such a sweet nature, is kind and generous to all. There is not a hint of pretension. She is humble and well-liked by everyone. And such a dutiful child! She frets about your well-being and is always wanting to send you some little thing. I have slipped this letter in with the gloves she asked me to post to you.

Mother Cleeve and Mary are also terribly fond of Emmie. She stops in at Bracken Brae every day to see Mother Cleeve and they chat up a storm about life in Canada. Emmie can hold her own in any conversation with the Cleeve men. She is quick to set them straight when they have difficulty remembering the lay of the land at their old home in the Eastern Townships of Quebec.

This morning when Dick the coachman was on his half day off, there was no one home to bring out the horse and buggy. Didn't Miss Emmie march out to the stable and hitch up the horse and buggy herself! My two girls wouldn't know the first thing about a horse, let alone which end of the buggy to hitch it to. You have done yourself proud in teaching her to cook and sew and tend the garden. She does up all the flowers in the house every morning. I dare say, she could manage an entire household if the need arose.

Tom is ever so impressed and has told me he would welcome

her with open arms if she were to come under our roof on a permanent basis. We are so looking forward to Frank's return from school next month. It would be wonderful if Frank and Emmie were to take to one another. But we will see what nature has in store.

If anything, Emmie is just a little too serious. Though I've no doubt it's due to her worries over the loss of the store. Tom tells her that misfortunes happen in business and that Willie and the boys will sort things out in due time. All of the Cleeve brothers agree that Willie will have turned things around in no time at all.

In the mean time, we are encouraging Emmie to rest up and get the colour back in her cheeks. She had such a dreadful cold after her crossing from Liverpool to Dublin. Dawse was so upset that he missed her arrival and was not able to get her to a hotel for the night. But Emmie has a very independent nature. Indeed she can well look after herself!

Emmie has been such wonderful company for me. With the children away at boarding school and Tom so often in London lately, it can get quite lonely here on my own. It has been a joy to have Emmie in the house. She plays the piano beautifully and we sing together on many an evening. She has also been so helpful with sewing rings on curtains and painting the lawn furniture during our re-decorating project.

I must say, that should Emmie end up staying with us, I would feel guilty for taking her away. I know how much she means to you all, especially you, dear Bel. Emmie is so capable around the house. With four boys to look after, I know how much you rely on your only daughter to help you through the endless list of daily chores. All the same, Willie is wise to insist that Emmie's future is secure. We cannot be selfish in keeping our children to ourselves. The day comes to us all when they must grow up and make their own way in life.

Eileen has her heart set on marrying her sweetheart, Sherrington Talbot. She wants to leave school at Christmas time and prepare for a June wedding next year. Wouldn't a double ceremony be wonderful! It would be just grand if you and Willie could come over for a fine celebration. Mind you, Tom wants Eileen to spend another year at school as he feels she's just too young to marry now. Men and their daughters!

Well, I must leave it at this. I hear Emmie calling me to get a move on or we will be late. We have an appointment in town with the dressmaker and then are off to the milliner. She is a handsome girl to start, and I want to gussie her up just a little for the upcoming social circuit.

Please give my best regards to Willie. Tom and I want you both to know that your precious child is well and we will take every care to see she is safe and that our little 'family plan' meets with success in due time.

I remain your dear cousin,

Phoebe Cleeve

~~~~~

FOUR

Life In Limerick

Cousin Mary Boyd Muses Over Wedding Bells in the Near Future

I can hear the church bells ringing at St. Munchin's across the way. Before long, there will be bells ringing for Dear Emmie and some fine young man! If it be God's will, (and Tom Cleeve's) that young man will be Frank Cleve. But I mustn't put the cart before the horse. We've got to get our sweet girl gussied up and ready for the summer social circuit. There's got to be an engagement before we can have a wedding! A little competition will only heighten the suspense.

To add some spice, Phoebe and I are overhauling Emmie's wardrobe. Perhaps they are a little more sedate in Canada when it comes to fashion. There is nothing wrong with being demure, I suppose. Playing the game of 'Hard to Get' never hurt, but there is nothing wrong with a little sugar to catch the attention of the flies. I have no doubt that with a nip and tuck here and a few flowers and ribbons there, Emmie will become an irresistible confection. She will have to beat the men away!

When Emmie was here today for tea, I could not help but remember when I was Bel's maid of honour. It seems like only yesterday! Now it is Bel's daughter's turn. My dear brother Tom has confided that he would be delighted to welcome Emmie as a permanent addition to his household. All the Cleeve boys agree that Emmie is a gem.

Frank will soon be taking on responsibilities in the business and he needs a good woman at his side. His days of lollygagging about and playing the field are numbered. Tom plans to have a 'man-to-man' chat about the importance of a mate and how to pick one. Yes, some fatherly advice will go a long way in getting Frank to take the matter seriously.

Mother Cleeve is so pleased. Indeed all the Cleeve women are excited to have a hand in our little family plot. Phoebe wants to please Tom and Mother Cleeve. And Kathleen says that even Jennie who has been so ill has perked up at the prospect of a family wedding. Mind you, Mother says that we mustn't count our chicks before they hatch. She insists that marriages are made in heaven and we don't want to pressure two young people into a match that is ill suited.

The two young people need some time to get to know one another. Frank will be home for the summer next month when school is out. It won't do any harm for Emmie to meet other young men in the mean time. After all, she needs to believe there is a field to choose from. If Frank is faced with some competition, that can only heighten his ardour as he cuts to the chase. And what a prize our Emmie will be!

I have to say that the girl is a tad shy. When the boys tease her about one young man or the other, she turns beet red and can only stammer and change the subject in a hurry. Well, she has been brought up well and is very innocent. I suppose that is as it should be. All the same, she doesn't seem to be quite 'on board' with this project. There is something that I cannot quite put my finger on that is amiss. Though I just can't imagine what that would be.

Perhaps Emmie just needs a mother to talk to. As Bel's oldest and dearest friend, I do hope she will come to confide in me. The good Lord has seen fit not to bless me with children, but that does not stop me from feeling the same maternal feelings that any mother has. Emmie is much loved and if anything at all is troubling her, I pray that she will come to me about it.

Bel says she will ask Edward to write to her and inquire if there is anything she would like to confide in him. They have always been devoted brother and sister. Bel believes they are very close, much more so than with any of the other boys. I well understand being the only girl amongst a passel of rough and tumble boys.

And I have to say that I do have a special place for my eldest brother Tom. Edward has not written to Emmie since she came to Ireland. She said only yesterday that she is disappointed and will write to scold him. Perhaps she misses him and a letter to let her know all is well at his new job will do the trick. Emmie does tend to fret about her loved ones.

Emmie Writes to Her Brother Edward

Sunville House

May 29th 1897.

My Dear Edward,

I thought before this I would have had a letter from you. I long to hear how you are getting along. Mother sends me word, all she knows. You would think it very funny to see how very demonstrative people are over here. Even Mary Boyd is a great softy with Jack. He is not as nice looking or as jolly as when I was here before. He has become fat and lazy.

When I laugh at Mary she says, "There is a good time coming for you and then Jack will have the laugh on you." She is very anxious to see me well dressed. I think she wants to get me married while I am in Ireland. In fact I think all my relations do, much to my amusement. They expect me to have a good time in August when the young people are home and the house is to be full of visitors. Until then I am just to get fat and strong. It is strange how very lazy I have grown, but not fat yet, although we are fed so well.

The Cleeve men work hard. Tom seldom gets home for dinner, and seven is the earliest he can get home, often it is nine. Fred gets up every morning at four or five and works before breakfast. His house is the nearest to the factory. Joe gets up at six. One of them is almost always on the road. Ted is living at Mallow now. He comes home every Saturday night.

I have got a pretty dress - black and white with small checks, and two blouses, one pink and the other mauve. Mary has trimmed my black hat with mauve, pink, and red hot ribbon so I am quite a swell.

Kathleen is a sweet little woman, rather pretty, very lady like looking. The eldest child Vera is plain but very sharp. She is like the Cleeves, particularly Mary. The baby is pretty, more like mother. Aylmer is a plain child; Charly is better looking. They are nice little fellows. Olive is very quiet. She has just got a musical Diploma for both violin and piano.

There are two pianos here, one upstairs, one down, so I can practice anywhere when the girls come home from school. The room I am in is a large bright room and is to be done up in white and gold, for the girls sitting room. The house is too big to be cozy but it is very nice, plenty of light and warm. Mary has the cosiest place, Fernbank, the best garden and stables, Beechlawn the prettiest grounds and finest trees, but Sunville is the swell place.

The view of the river from here is grand. We see all the ships and boats that come in to dock. There are two tennis courts here, one at the other houses. Cousin Tom is going to join the Club Tennis Court, as all the gay people go to it. They play twice a week, he thinks.

Tom is like a father to me. He pets me and is so kind. Indeed where I am made so much of, I cannot be homesick. I must stop now as we are going over to see Mary. With much love and good wishes for your work.

Ever your loving sister,

Emily.

Becoming One of the Family

Sunville House

May 31 1897

My Darling Mother,

I wonder if this has been as long a month to you as to me. I seem to have seen so much and met many people. I hope you got the veil and gloves O.K. Tell me if they were all right. Yesterday we went to church in the morning. I wore my new shirt and Mary's silk waist. Mary trimmed my hat on Saturday with the ribbon. Mrs. Bernard gave me some silk and flowers she bought in town for me. I also wore the long gold chain that belonged to grandmother French. Long chains are the fashion and Mary says I must wear it. Many have admired it.

The afternoon and evening were so wet that, except between showers when we went to Fernbank, we did not go out. Do not tell this till you hear more, but Jennie Cleeve is going to London to be operated on. She is all wrong inside. Aunt Cleeve and Mary Journeaux do not know this so be careful to say nothing in your letters to worry them.

We spent the evening talking about home before the fire in big stuffed arm chairs. This morning I washed my head as I could not do it before due to my cold. I helped to make lace curtains, and after dinner we hung them. At five I went over to see Aunt for a few minutes, returning at seven. It is now half past, we will have tea at eight. It is as light now as it has been all day. Ever since last Monday it has rained off and on every day.

Next Monday Cousin Tom is going to take a holiday. Saturday will be his birthday and he will take us off on some trip. Now I hope the weather will be fine. Saturday will be Tom, Fred, Aylmer, and Charly's birthdays; Sunday Aunt Sophia's. I must get her some little thing.

June 1st

Yesterday was Mrs. Tom's day at home, but as there was a choral service at the Cathedral, we went to it at three. The music was fine but very loud. I like the Cathedral choir alone better. After we got home Kathleen Cleeve and a Miss Katy Aston called. She came over from England yesterday and is an old school friend of Kathleen's. Miss Aston is taller than me, nice looking and about twenty- three or so. She played most of the evening and is a great musician.

The horse and trap went over to Bracken Brae to collect Aunt Sophia and Mary. They stayed at Sunville until near seven. I had just taken off my day dress and put on my silk waist and sat down to the piano. We sang and had a jolly time. Later, Phoebe walked over to Bracken Brae with Aunt Sophia, but my hip was not well, so I did not go.

Mr. Hudson, the clergyman out where the Dann's used to live, came to call. (When I was here before, he was curate at the Cathedral.) We talked until eight, when we then had tea. Mr. Hudson spent three years in Upper Canada twelve years ago.

After tea we sat out on the steps until the three "Beechlawns" and Mary and Jack came over when we went in. Mr. Hudson slept here all night as he had to go away by an early train and will stay here tonight again, returning home tomorrow. About half past nine Cousin Tom came in and I gave him his tea. I am quite like a daughter in the house.

I have just been moving my things to a big room in the front of the house, the one Mrs. Thompson had. Phoebe thought it was lonely for me in the "Bachelor's quarters". That is what they call the part of the house where I was at first. I am sorry to go, for although the room is smaller and has only one window, it was very cozy and I liked being opposite the bathroom.

June 4

Workmen in Ireland are very slow. Two men have been here ten days painting and papering three rooms and they are not finished yet. Yesterday we chose a carpet for the breakfast room which has been done up. It is a light Brussels. Most of the carpets here are velvet, but I advised Mrs. Tom to get Brussels, as the room is small and will look cleaner, more suitable for a morning room.

Yesterday, I crocheted a toilet cover for Mrs. Tom. Then we went to a very interesting meeting about getting Jubilee nurses in Limerick. We called at Beechlawn and Fernbank on our way back. We did not go out in the evening though as it was after ten when Cousin Tom got home and too late after he had had his tea.

Today, Dick drove me to Bracken Brae for lunch and Mrs. Tom called for me at four, when we went into town. I got lining to make up the white musveiling dress. I will make the skirt myself and get the waist made at the dressmaker's. It is for evening but will be high necked. I have made my black dress short to wear with blouses and bound it with braid. I send you a piece to see; it is very nice. I have taken the sleeves out of my white muslin jacket and made them smaller. Now the cook is washing it and I will do it up later.

Phoebe is calling me so I must go. Please kiss father and the boys for me.

Ever your loving daughter.

Emily Woodburn

A Grand Pic Nic to the Clare Glen

Sunville House

June 8th 1897

My Darling Dad,

I am going to write you an account of a lovely picnic we took yesterday. On account of the two girls (Miss Aston and Miss Woodburn), Tom and Joe decided to take a half holiday. So at twelve o'clock, Joe, Kathleen and Miss Aston left Beechlawn. Joe, with his man and the baskets, was driving a fine pair of red horses the colour of our Jack.

Tom, Phoebe, Olive and me were in the Wagonette with Dick in livery. With many boxes, baskets and the boot piled with bottles, we set out for Clare Glen. (I had better tell what I wore as mother says I must tell every little thing. I looked quite fine in my old black skirt, white blouse, black belt and gloves, plaid tie and sailor hat.)

We drove through the Irish town, past the new Reservoir which is near Troy Castle and Castle Connell. We passed the Masterson's and Baunaline's lovely residences, over the lovely little Annacotty bridge, past the Annacotty grist Mill to Annagh Factory. This is a new factory the Cleeves have just put up where the milk from fifty farmers is brought and separated and then the cream is driven to Limerick Factory. The milk is returned to the farmers as the Cleeves only buy the cream.

Photo taken in 1897 with Joe Cleeve's home camera. From left to right: Phoebe Cleeve, Emmie, Katy Aston, Kathleen Cleeve, Tom Cleeve, and Olive Cleeve in front.

At two o'clock we set our table beside a lovely brook, when down came the rain. So we hurried into the factory and finished our lunch standing. At three we started off again, the rain only lasting for a few minutes. We journeyed over lovely winding roads where the trees, their trunks covered with ivy, and leafy branches overhead give shade. We finally reached the Glen where many cars and carriages were standing. Two old women, with many blessings for the silver coins we gave them, let us in the gates.

Oh how lovely it was! We walked up the lovely glen, and across the stile, through the little meadow to the Second Glen which is quite as beautiful as the first. We crossed a new little stone bridge to the falls where we sat and talked for a long while. I have enclosed some heather from the Glen.

The lovely Rhododendrons were in flower and the gorse made the warm bright air sweet. The shades and shadows were grand, but you know all dear Father, so why would I try to describe? Joe brought his Camera. I hope he will give me some snaps to send to you. Except for Tom and Joe, none of us had seen the Glen before.

At six we started back again and had tea in the factory where we left our things, the kettle being boiled near by. While we were there, the milk came in, so we saw them separate it and we drank fresh cream with our tea. At Castle Troy the rain came down fast for a few minutes, but we had plenty of wraps. At half past nine we got in to Limerick, and stopped at Fernbank to let Olive out. We were all tired when we got home.

I would have gone to bed only I always take charge of boiling the little spirit lamp and making the punch. I also lock up the pantry and turn off the gas. We went to bed early at half past ten and I did not stir till hot water was brought to me by the maid at a quarter past eight. This morning we did not have breakfast till nine.

I have been telephoning over to Beechlawn to say that although this is Tuesday, we are not receiving callers today. As the day is wet, Cousin Phoebe has the drawing room upside down, also the remainder of the house. I have been cleaning most of the morning and afternoon. The maid and I sewed rings on the curtains for the drawing room. The workmen will finish tomorrow.

I had a nice letter from Miss Butler Saturday, asking me to visit them whenever I like. At noon I had such a nice letter from Mrs. Devereaux, giving me a description of the places she had seen since she went to London. Her brother has a swell place in Hampstead, London. (Mrs. Tom says that is a lovely part of the city.) It was good of her to write. I wish I could send her letter home but it is too long and heavy.

June 10th

I saw the outside of the poor old County Gaol yesterday where grandfather was gaol keeper. It is dreadfully run down now. Do you remember above the gaol there was a field? Well there is a row of fine brick houses being built as well as on the empty space a little higher up. (On the other side of William Street.)

I will write to Edward and Dick by this mail as well. Kiss Harry and Ben for me.

With much love, dear old Dad.
Your loving child Emmie

~~~~~

FIVE

On The Subject Of Men And Marriage

Brother Edward Broaches A Delicate Subject

"My Dearest Sister Emmie –" Ah, what shall I say to her? I'm beginning to wish Mother hadn't asked me to take on the task of talking some sense into the dear girl. Yes, Em and I have always shared a special bond, but surely marriage is a topic to be discussed between mother and daughter.

I hardly know where to begin, or how for that matter. My only sister has always been such a headstrong girl. I don't want to be too blunt and send her reeling in the opposite direction. Then Edward will be blamed for spoiling the entire plan. No we can't have that!

Mother seemed awfully anxious in her letter this week. I dare say she is desperate. She fears that dear Em will never come round. She says it's a bad sign that Em has shown no interest in courting and at twenty-three is just about on the shelf. I must write to Mother and remind her that she was nearly twenty-eight years of age when she and Papa tied the knot. I'm sure that all this worry is for naught.

Emmie is just shy and perhaps a little over sensitive. I've no doubt that Father is right when he says that the local prospects are too rough for our Em. She just hasn't met up with the right sort of young men. Besides, her health can be a little delicate. (I hope that pain in her side is not still troubling her. I thought she ought to see the doctor about it, but Papa didn't think it was anything to worry about. She just needs to get married and the benefits of motherhood will set her right.)

I don't want her to get the impression that we are trying to pawn her off. Surely she knows how precious she is to me, indeed to us all. It's strictly a practical matter. Even if Papa does find work soon, he won't be around forever and I, as the eldest son can barely feed myself. It will be some time before the younger boys could help out and I suppose they will eventually have families of their own to support. I can't bear the thought of Emmie being forced to take on some lowly profession as a dressmaker or housekeeper to some cranky old widower just to keep the wolf from the door. No, there is no other solution. While she is in Ireland, Emmie must find a husband of good Irish stock, just like our Papa.

Now, how can I put this to Em delicately? She has always been such a kind and generous girl. Perhaps I can appeal to that part of her character. "Wouldn't you like someone in your life who is dearer than a brother, someone special to love?" Yes, that's it. She always sets herself aside for others. She is tireless in her attentions to Mama and the boys and should Papa need anything at all, Emmie is the first one there to meet the needs of the occasion. It's no wonder we call her 'Our Darling', for I have never met such a sweet, kind and loving girl as my sister Emily.

God, I am homesick. It's been almost three months now since I packed my bags and left Melbourne. Mind you, I do enjoy seeing a bit of the world, even if it's only as far as Ontario. Kingston is a grand place and I do love the boating in these parts. Maybe I could follow in grandfather Woodburn's footsteps and find employment at the local gaol. Wouldn't father be tickled at that! They do say that 'what's bred in the bone is born in the flesh'. Perhaps I might one day be Keeper of the gaol, just like my old grandpapa.

But, I do long for the good old days before that dreadful fire when we were all together and enjoying the life of a good, hard working Christian family. Perhaps it is our time to be tested. The Lord giveth and the Lord taketh away. The loss of the store has ruined us. Now Father, Dick and I are scattered in separate directions as we seek honest work. Emmie has been sent across the ocean to find a husband.

Perhaps worst of all, poor Mother is left alone at home to fend for herself and the two young boys. She has such a heavy load to carry without us. That reminds me - soon it will be time to put in the garden. I must arrange to get back home for the May 24th weekend to help with the planting. I doubt that Father will get there.

Well, all this worry isn't going to help. I must get on with this letter to Em. Longing for our childhood days is not going to change anything. Em and I are grown-ups now and we must get on with the life of men and women. That sounds so serious. Perhaps she will laugh at me if I say that. After all, we are brother and sister and will always think of each other as childhood chums.

I must write something cheery so it doesn't sound like life is all doom and gloom. I can tell Em all about the lovely scenery around Kingston and of course about the lakes and boating. She will enjoy hearing that the boarding house where I am staying has a canoe as well as a row boat. Even though the Spring weather is a little chilly yet, the paddling is great fun- as long as I don't come a cropper with a large rock and end up capsized!

Emmie Replies to Her Brother Edward

Sunville House

June 10th 1897

My Darling Edward,

I was so pleased to get your letter of the 30th from Kingston today. Aunt sent it down from Dublin. I was only there 10 days. I am so glad you enjoyed your paddle. Going about will do you good. It is well for people who can to travel and see a bit of the world. I am sure the scenery you have so nicely described would be lovely. I am also enjoying beautiful views.

It seems more than three months since I saw you dear old man and now for your question. Do I ever wish for anyone dearer than a brother? No, not if I could always have you who I so much love. Dear me, for I have always told you, my best loved brother, all my thoughts, but I hate to think you are homesick and alone. I wish I could comfort you. My heart is large and warm for those at home, but I never saw a man I cared to see again, except as a friend. And I have met a good many men, but perhaps dear old fellow, I am cold, but never to those I love.

You being a bit older than me, perhaps feel the want of someone of your own to love. No I did not laugh at your letter. It made me sad and homesick, (the first time I have been homesick since I left home) - to think I could not be all in all to you. Though separated by the mighty ocean, you are always in my thoughts and often do I pray God Almighty to bless, guide and keep you. Yes, we are men and women done with childhood days.

How I wish father had work. I find it hard to be bright when I think of things at home. I feel as if I must be there to help. I do try to write bright letters to them all and pray that God keeps them safe.

Everyone is very kind to me here; of course it is quiet as Phoebe and I are much alone. Cousin Tom never comes home to dinner, and it is eight or nine at night before he leaves work. The Cleeve boys are very busy now. The Jubilee gives them increased orders. Cousin Phoebe works hard, for she has a very large house and only three servants. She needs four for the size, as everything is kept in beautiful order.

I am quite like a daughter here. I have the run of different places and charge of one thing and another. Every morning, first thing, I do all the flowers in the house, there are about twenty bowls filled with roses and all kinds of colourful blooms. I have to keep them fresh. It takes me from one to two hours to gather and arrange all.

Then Aunt Sophia likes to see me, so nearly every day I go over to Bracken Brae which is half a mile from Sunville. Beechlawn is next door to Sunville while Fernbank is half a mile nearer to town. But as all these houses are on a circular road, Aunt Sophia is only equal distance from Fernbank and Sunville. Indeed, Aunt is a wonderful old woman, so bright and active and proud of her children. She is very fond of me.

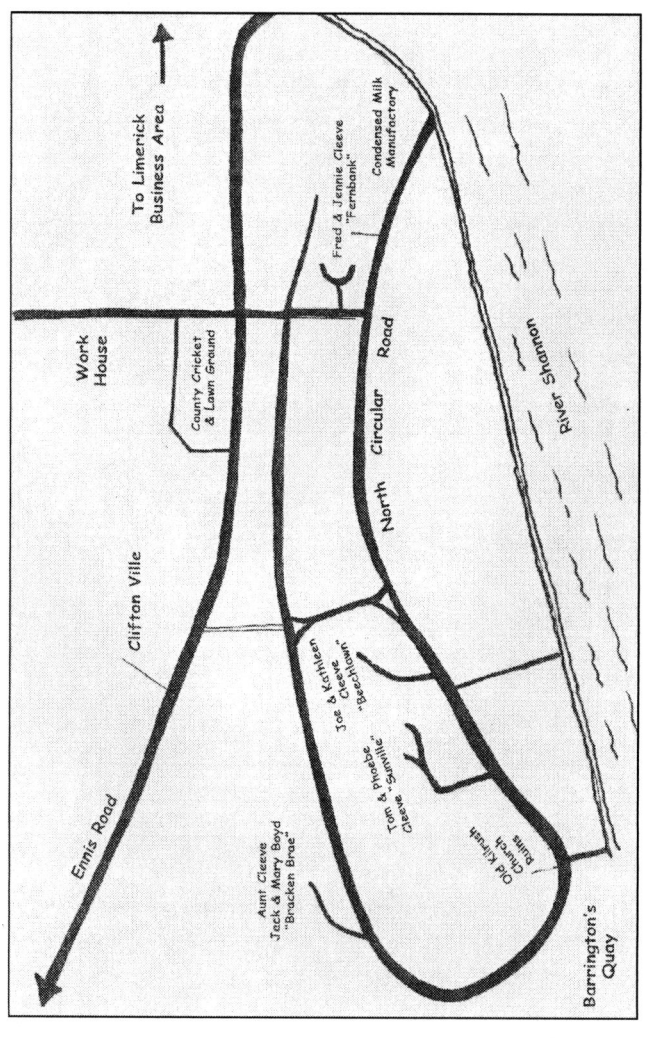

NORTH CIRCULAR ROAD, LIMERICK

The Cleeves are turning out ten ton of butter in a week. They have 800 hands here, 300 in Mallow where Ted is living now. He comes home every Saturday night. The Beechlawns and we three with Olive went for a lovely picnic on Whit Monday, a holiday, to a lovely Glen called Clare. It is about ten miles from Limerick. Although a lovely country, the Glen is about five miles long. We left here at twelve, stopped at two at a factory of the Cleeves in Annagh for lunch, and returned here at seven for tea, the kettle being boiled in a hut near by. It was near ten when we got home. Both Beechlawn and Sunville drove a pair. Wednesday, Joe took me, also a friend of Kathleen's, a Miss Aston, an English girl, to the annual Sports held in large grounds near the gaol on William Street.

I met several I knew, among them Mr. Masterson, who said he was charmed to meet me, and brought his two sons up to introduce to me, one 27, the other 31. They are rather like the father, the youngest is rather the nicer. They are lazy, have more money than brains. I fancy it was after six when we left there. There were Bike races, men and boys running and jumping etc. It was very good and the prizes were grand. We sat near them on the Grand Stand. Of course there was a police guard nearby, and they were railed off from the people. Although the day was very dull, like rain, everyone wore their best bib and tucker. There was a crowd of many hundreds. I did not know any women but met five men I knew. Indeed my Limerick acquaintances are mostly men.

Amongst the ladies I like Joe's wife, Kathleen, best. She is so very sweet. Her eldest child is very plain, quite like Mary with such a curly head. The baby is pretty, like her mother. At Beechlawn, she has five servants. (Sunville and Fernbank have six each.) The

Fernbanks have far the best gardens. Their pears, peaches, and apples last them till Xmas and they have small fruit in plenty.

There is to be a Jubilee service here on Sunday week. The music will be the same as that at St. Paul's on the twenty-second. Among the stringed instruments, Kathleen and Olive are to play violins. There is also to be a Royal Military band. I suppose the Cathedral will be crowded. The service is to be at three in the afternoon and I expect all the Cleeves will attend.

Fred Cleeve's wife, Jennie, is very delicate so she may not come. She has had three operations and is still in bed. Her daughter, Olive, is very quiet; also the boys- they are plain little fellows.

I have been making a dress this morning (white). Phoebe said she would just as soon eat it as make it. She pays from 30-55 dollars for all of her dresses. They are silk lined. But for all this, she is pretty close. Nothing is wasted or spent that can be helped, but there is a good woman. Eileen will be eighteen next Spring in February, and she is very anxious to leave school at Christmas. I think she will. Cecil is at school near Dublin. He is the only one of the children I have seen. He is a very bad boy, but has taken a fancy to me. I regret to say his parents spoil him, never refuse him money, or anything. I must stop now. It is dinner time.

God bless you and prosper you. Your loving sister,

Emily Woodburn

Something Wrong in my Composition

Sunville House

June 13 1897

My Darling Mother,

On Saturday afternoon after I mailed my letters, Cousin Phoebe took Mrs. Baylor and me to see the boys of all the church choirs in the sporting event. There was running, jumping, and military drill. The sports were held in the lovely grounds across the river opposite Sunville, Mr Bannantine's. We sat under the trees on chairs. We left Sunville at three, returning at five. The games were not over then but Mrs. B. was tired. The prizes were lovely and there was a tent for afternoon tea. The day was fine but dull, like the sports on Thursday, but about eight o'clock down came the rain for the night.

Yesterday we all went to church. I wore my black skirt and Mary's silk jacket. I fixed it up a bit, so have it for a time for best, gray gloves, and my black hat with white veil. As it was Trinity Sunday, we remained for Communion. How I longed to be kneeling beside you there, dear Mother, instead of between my kind cousins. After dinner we were walking about, when Mrs. Baylor said, "I wish I could see the Dann's old house." So Cousin Phoebe said, "Why we might drive out now!" (It is where she grew up.)

So the ponies were put in and off we went at four, through Limerick, up the river wash, past Lord Emly's. Then we passed the old church where little May Cleeve and grandmother Dann are buried, and then on to the lovely old Rectory. It is sadly out of repair, the grounds are overgrown, but it would take a good private purse to keep the mile of shrubbery walk, tennis courts, two drives, lawns, meadow, and out buildings in repair. The last time I was there was to say goodbye to the Dann's. It made me feel quite sad as the big house has been shut up since. But we got a key from the cottage lodger and went all over the property.

It was after eight when we got back to Sunville and nine when we had tea. Then Tom and Phoebe went down to see Jennie Cleeve at Fernbank. Mrs. Baylor and I kept house. We ate our supper at eleven and I locked up and off we went to bed. It was twelve when Tom and Phoebe came in with the latchkey. I went to sleep then with an easy conscience.

Mrs Baylor and I get on well. She gave me a pretty pair of cuff links yesterday, just what I wanted. She says I am too ready to run for people, that I must let others wait on me or I will never get fat. She is old, about 60 or 64, I would guess. I always get on well with old people, much better than with the young.

Mrs. B. says I am the most steady sober girl for my age that she knows and I need to liven up. Phoebe says when the house is full next month, I will not have time to be quiet and will grow young. Tomorrow we are to have a tea party. It will be tennis in the afternoon, tea and billiards in the evening. This afternoon we are to go to the tennis club as the day is lovely.

I am going over to see Aunt Sophia at twelve as Mary will not be home till evening. Aunt will be a bit lonely. Today I will walk over as my hip is much better this last week, but I cannot play tennis yet. It is too bad! Kathleen and Miss Aston go to the club almost every day and I could go with them, for there are three ladies days there. (I need to walk, for I have cramps, and have now been six weeks overdue since the first of May, on the "Vancouver".)

Wednesday 15th.

I have just got your P.S. and papers dear Mother. I was disappointed at not getting a letter. But I guess you are awfully busy. I suppose the reason the boys have left school is that the June fees were a stumbling block. Do make them help you well dear mother, for I am anxious about you. In the paper there is the account of the death of a James Stevens, 23. Is that the nice looking boy who was at college a few years ago, living near the Kirkdale Church and was at the Matthias' for dinner last summer?

It is dreadfully cold today here. I can hardly hold the pen, my fingers are so stiff. It rained hard all day yesterday, so no tennis. There were a few visitors, three men, Miss Aston, Miss Haddlesy, and Joe for tea. We had music, then some of the men went to the Billiard Room, and Mrs. Tom, Miss Haddlesy, Joe and I fought when we played whist. I think there must be something wrong in my composition, for I do not get on well with young men, only old men and women.

The night was so stormy, Mr. Fogarty and Mr. Hudson remained all night. They left with Tom a few minutes ago. Mr. Hudson was here the night before and all day yesterday. I do not like him as well as I did. I simply cannot get on well with young men.

Mary did not come home from Kilkee till yesterday so it is a good thing I went in to see Aunt Sophia. I will go and see them this afternoon. This morning I am going in to town to get a new white hat and the waist of the white dress made. The skirt I am making looks nice. We are to go at twelve; it is eleven now.

How is the garden getting on, are the flowers good this year? I suppose there are very few vegetables yet. We have all kinds here. You have not told me how your satin dress looks. Did Miss Armstrong do it nicely? And do you like the little veil I sent from Dublin?

I have heard that Mat Aylmer is in England. We saw an account of his leaving and arriving in the Cork paper. Aunt Sophia is in a great state of excitement about it. If he does not come over to Ireland she will have a fit.

I have not heard from Mrs. Rainback. Perhaps she will not ask me to visit. If I had an invitation, I was in hopes Tom would take me over with him next month when he gets the girls from school. But Phoebe would be lonely. She says she does not know what she would do without me. The house is cleaned, carpets and curtains hung by men from town. I have done quite a lot of sewing for Phoebe. She does not care for fussy work, so I have fixed a few things for her.

Thursday 16th

I got a hat, a fancy white one trimmed with Chiffon, leaves of ivy, and a pink flower. I think it is too big and fine for me, but it is Mrs. Tom's choice. She wants me to be well dressed. I paid 2 ½ for it (two dollars and a half) and I left the white dress waist at the dressmakers to be done up.

It rained all day yesterday so we were not long in town. Today has also been wet, the fifth wet day together, so I finished my white skirt. It looks very nice indeed and I had no trouble with it. I have been outdoors all afternoon and painted some tables for Phoebe while she did some flower stands.

Then we walked down to Fred's to see Jennie. She is better, still in bed, though. Then we went on to Bracken Brae. Mary enjoyed her visit to Kilkee very much. She is suffering with rheumatism in her arms.

Saturday June 19th

Yesterday was dreadfully wet, also today. I went into town with Mary to do some shopping and then returned with her for lunch at Bracken Brae. Aunt Sophia was pleased to see me and expects to see me every day. I was very wet and had all my heavy clothes on. Had to dry off at the kitchen fire, and was cold as an iceberg, indeed. Sunville has open windows in every direction. The last four evenings we have had a fire in the upstairs sitting room.

Last night we all went over to Beechlawn. While the others were putting on their things, Joe called me into the dining room and said, "I want to give you some little thing, and Kathleen did not know what you wanted, so I thought you could get what you wanted yourself." He gave me a pound or $5. I did not like to take it but he insisted. I will put it to general things, nothing particularly. (Ask father if he remembers if the Cheque Tom sent me to come over to Ireland on, was from J.P. Evans or Cleeve Brothers. He keeps asking so I am anxious to find out but I cannot think why he wants to know.)

The horse show is to be held next week. Everyone is talking about it. We are to go as it is one of the yearly Limerick events and everyone has a new turnout for the occasion. Dawse and Ruth go up to London today, on the Jubilee. They have a club window, to see the lights from, and must be there at six o'clock in the morning Tuesday. Everyone is all excited about the event. If the weather does not improve, it will not be much pleasure in the dreadful crush. Aunt Journeaux is in London and wrote to Aunt Cleeve that Mrs. Rainback is very ill; no hope of her recovery, so I will not be asked there.

Uncle Ben writes to me every few days. If Mrs. Wright cannot go up to Dublin, I will offer to stay with Aunt while he comes down. He is most anxious to come to Limerick next month. I have been here four weeks Thursday and they are just as kind to me as ever.

Yesterday a shipload of timber was chartered from India for Cleeve Brothers. It will arrive here the end of next month. They get two loads every year. They turn out ten ton of butter a day, six in Limerick. Ted has left Mallow for the present. He is glad to get home.

I have just had Canada letters from Ethel and Miss Bernard. Miss B. says she has been very ill and that you went over to see her, also that you were looking well. I worry when you look ill; if she said you looked badly, I should have had such a fright. I would have gone home by the first boat.

Tell Lord Aylmer that Aunt Sophia says Miss Mack has not forgotten his last kiss. She is still in Mallow, very happy in her new home. (She has been governess here for two years and has gone to Mallow for the same purpose.) She was here at Sunville for several days after I came down from Dublin. Molly Wright is ill. They are all very delicate. Joe will never be well and may die any time. Fran is also weak and the two little ones are sickly. Poor Mrs. Wright! What a lot of trouble she has had since Ben's wife is dead.

I am longing for a home letter, a P.S. does not hold much, but

I know how busy you are dear mother. I must close now and get this letter down to the pillar. I always mail on Saturday, so when letters are late it is the fault of the steamers. The weather has been so rough at sea, that many boats have been late and this week, five vessels were sunk in the channel, one with all hands on board off Belfast. I came over in a good time. Please kiss dear father and the boys for me.

Ever my dear little Mother. Your loving child.

Emily Woodburn

~~~~

SIX

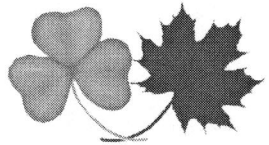

Diamond Jubilee Celebrations

Jubilee Week

Sunville House

June 23rd 1897

My Own Dear Father,

Thanks for the papers; June 4 & 11 came in a few minutes ago. I will send them on to Dublin. I see that Henry Aylmer has gone into mining. I do hope it will be a success but I hate those sort of things. They can be so unpredictable! I have written to Arthur Aylmer by this mail for his birthday and to congratulate him on passing his exam.

The weather here is dreadfully wet, only one fine day in three weeks. Monday it misted all day. In the morning I went into town with Mary and she asked me to go back with her to spend the day at Bracken Brae. Phoebe did not want me to go, as she had planned for a drive in the countryside. She said we had been indoors too much due to the weather.

Phoebe is most anxious to make me fat and for me to enjoy myself. Well not fat, only a little more flesh and colour. She likes people to be thin. Mary said she spoke most affectionately of me to her on Sunday.

After dinner we three went off to town. First we did a bit of shopping and then picked up Mrs. Baylor who bought me some lovely sweets. (I wish I could send the boys some but it would cost too much in postage.) Then we drove out by Corbally, down a lovely lane, and home by St. Munchin's, and the Workhouse.

We were out until after seven. It was lovely. The rain was so slight that we did not get damp. The old Mill is looking a bit shaky, and as the tide was out, the lovely river did not look its best. Many of the houses had flags flying for the Jubilee. At Uncle Eddy Hosford's in Corbally there were grand decorations and great strings of flags. He called out to Mrs. Tom as we drove past.

Yesterday was the great Jubilee day. It was fine until eight, then there began a mist which is still continuing. We decided on Monday evening that it would be nice to go to Killaloe, so Tom asked Ted and Miss Aston to join us. Joe could not leave and Kathleen was not well. So we called for Olive and Mrs. Fogarty and we all left by train at eleven. We got a first class carriage to ourselves, and as the men decided the lake would be the nicest place to do, they telegraphed to Killaloe to hold the little steamer called "Lady of the Lake" for a party from Limerick.

The steamer only holds twelve, so as we were nine, no one else was allowed on board. When the train stopped, Cousin Tom found that we could get no grub on board, so he bought some biscuits, cheese, bread and sardines which we ate very picnic style, without plates and in the principle that thumbs were made before spoons or forks. (We all had pen knives.)

The train took us a quarter of a mile below the station to the quay where we embarked. The water was lovely, the scene divine. We steamed down that lovely lake and up such a very narrow winding river, about two miles long to the village of Scarrif. It was two o'clock when we stopped and made our way to the funny little houses in search of a hotel. There was only one and a party was there before us, so we started up the village street, which is built up a hill, one house or hut a bit higher than the last. What a novel scene it presented!

It was fair day and the cattle were lying in the street, men shouting, dogs barking. As to dogs, I never saw so many anywhere. They were all sorts and condition of dogs, and strange to say all were muzzled. As we came up some dogs set on to a poor little fellow who could not fend them off. Well Mr. Fogarty came to the rescue and broke his umbrella on the dogs.

At the top of this hill was a sort of square, or open space, where carts, horses, people, not to speak of cows, calves, pigs, sheep etc. were in grand confusion. People looked out from every door and window as we came up. It seems it was a novelty to see so many strangers in so remote a spot, for few visit it. (Did you ever?) None of our party was ever there before.

We made enquiries but could not find another hotel. There was a boarding house of only three rooms where they said they could give us food. But they had no turf to make a fire so could not cook it. So we abandoned that strange street, such a place as I never expect to see again.

We returned to the hotel, where we sat on the fence opposite, or rather on a wall. Four bicyclists had been there and had eaten all the meat and bread to be had in the place. But after about an hour we got some fresh hot bread, plenty of fried eggs, a little ham, with plenty of butter, weak tea (minus the sugar) and skim milk.

However, as we were very jolly, no one minded. Then, in the middle of this strange repast, the steamer whistled for us, so we had to run with our mouths full. Off we went amid the cheers of small boys, and the grand performance of a Mountebank. (There had been plenty of beer and whiskey at the hotel, so on the boat Ted was very jolly, which was horrid.)

The boat stopped at Mount Shannon, took off a load and one passenger and then we started back to town. The wind had got up, so we had quite a swell, as the lake you know is quite big, and being land-locked holds all the breeze. It was lovely with the grand hills all around us, beautifully green, with the white houses scattered about.

It was after seven when we got to the quay again. The train was waiting for us and, what a time we had getting off and on her. There is no platform, as the train only unloads luggage at the quay for Mount Shannon or Scarriff. A trainman got into the carriage and with one man hoisting from below with Ted, Tom lifted and pulled us up into the train.

It was eight when we arrived in Limerick. Dick had the carriage ready for us and we hurried home where we ate a much-needed dinner. Then we dressed up for the "Military Tattoo" over at the barracks. Such a crowd there was! All the Cleeves turned out except Jennie, and there were six visitors. We all drove up together and so were a huge party by ourselves.

The Tattoo was a torch light procession with all kinds of brass and stringed instruments that played beautifully. There were also fireworks and illuminations in the big square. Seats were placed about so people could sit down when tired of promenading. Of course we met many we knew, as there were several thousands. The square is enormous and as there are about 600 soldiers quartered here all the time with their families, they are a world by themselves. It was fine to see all the windows blazing.

As we drove through the town, we met a "Rebel lot of Rabble", (the bad Irish, about 200 to 300 strong.) They had a cart on which was a black coffin and a black flag, on which in white was written "Long live Old Ireland, down with the queen, who does nothing for us". They were pretty quiet for so many, but as our ponies were restless, we turned down the street. This was the only fuss we saw all day, not much for Old Ireland.

From all public buildings flags were flying. The Cleeve Factory had strings of them. The ships in dock were gay with flags and bunting. Many houses and buildings were illuminated. So the town was wonderfully gay.

Tom and a few of the Circular Road people are going to have fireworks on the river (on a barge) opposite T.H. Cleeve's lovely residence, the best on the Circular Road. Ten pounds have been spent on the fireworks! They are to be shown off tomorrow night after the Horse Show. A party is to come back from the Horse Show with us and we are to have dinner (very swell) at eight. After that, the fireworks will be set off. I will finish this when I can tell about it tomorrow.

Friday 25th

Great disappointment! The fireworks which were to come from London for last night never turned up. Four people had been asked out for dinner after the Horse Show to see them. However, the dinner was a success, and we had music, and walked about the grounds. It is daylight here until ten o'clock now, so after dinner we had coffee under the trees.

I had charge of the little arrangements and Mrs. Fogarty said to Cousin Phoebe,

" Miss Woodburn takes the place of your daughter here." Cousin Phoebe replied, " She is much better. She can do anything and is so thoughtful. The girls know nothing about housekeeping. I do not know what I would do without her." I need not say that I was greatly pleased. Then Tom said, "If any man wants a wife, he could not get a better or more useful one." This was rather embarrassing to say the least.

Cousin Kathleen told me she thought the new white hat I wore at the Horse Show was one of the prettiest hats of the season and most becoming, so I felt very well pleased with it after that. Now I am sending you a paper with an article about the show, which will tell you about the jumping etc.

It was most exciting and interesting. There was a hedge and ditch, two sorts of banks, and a water jump and stone wall. Seventy jumped and only two men were thrown. They were not hurt and mounted again. Some of the horses that were good hunters refused to jump three times in a row. They were excited by the band and crowds. We had seats on the grand stand and, at five, had tea and cake in a tent near by. I enjoyed the show very much. The show dogs were nice and flowers very fine.

Saturday 26th

The Show was continued yesterday but Mrs. Baylor was too tired to go. Joe asked me to go with them, but I thought I had better not stand too much as my hip was aching. So, in the afternoon, we went for a lovely drive, out the Ennis Road almost to Cracklow, then home by the Police Barracks turn. That brought us out below the Workhouse.

The day was lovely and warm so we enjoyed it very much. After tea we walked about the grounds a bit, and then Tom and I went over to Beechlawn. Fred and Miss Haddlsey, also Aunt Sophia and Mary were there for a little. They played Billiards. I only talked as I do not play. We stayed very late till ten to twelve. When we got in, we found Phoebe and Mrs. Baylor had gone to bed.

In the morning, I went in to Town and did some shopping - collars, cuffs, veil, white sailor hat, a pair of stout boots for bad weather, and tan shoes and stockings for best with light clothes. I paid four dollars for the boots, three for the shoes, and this was at a cheap sale! But leather is high here and Mrs. Tom likes me to get good things. Mary says I must please her as much as possible!

I must stop this epistle now and get it out to the post. I have baked a cake and this afternoon will take it over to Bracken Brae, as it is Mary's day to receive callers. Of course it is wet, but we have had two fine days. Please give my love to Ben and Harry.

Ever my dear Dad,
Your Loving Child,

Emily

The Limerick Social Circuit Is Underway

Sunville House

July 4th 1897 Sunday

My Darling Mother,

Yesterday morning I walked down to the Pillar with your letter to post and then Cousin Phoebe and I went over to Bracken Brae. Just at the gate, we met the postman and he gave me your long letter and a newspaper from father. So at Bracken, I read your letter and then read parts of it to Aunt Sophia. She said to tell you that that was what she called a letter, and that she thought you were a good mother to write so much. I told her I deserved it all, as I wrote long ones home and you had not written a letter for two weeks, but just put me off with a P.S.

I am so glad the boys got to Montreal for the Jubilee. It will be something to remember all their lives with Father. It was good of Aunt Em to stay with you the night you were alone. I would have been very anxious about you if you were all alone, poor little Mother. It makes me feel dreadfully to think you are so much alone. I feel as if I must go home at once and take care of my dear little Mother. Be sure and tell me every time you write how you are and if you want me to go home. Remember I will go any day you send for me.

Mrs. Lodge said I should love to have Emmie live with me always, but I refused at once. I am Mother's girl and will not leave my home for all the old women in the world, unless Father turns me out. But, Please God, he will get some good job and we will be all together again. I find I am a home bird.

Cousin Phoebe sends you her love and says to say that you have brought me up well, that I am a good child, and very useful and that she is very fond of me. She is very sweet in her manner to me and introduces me to her friends as " My cousin Miss Woodburn".

We were at church this morning and, as it was fine, I wore my new dress. Everyone said it looked nice. Tom said he was proud of me. I had the silk lace Grandmother gave me around the neck and sleeves, under which is green ribbon like Juniper, also around my waist finishing in a bow at the back. I wore the big white hat with pink and green trim, tan shoes and stockings, tan gloves and green silk parasol.

I will wear this dress a good bit this week, as it is to be a gay one. There is a party here Tuesday, Fogarty's Wednesday, and garden party at the Dean of Limerick's Friday. You know the piece of white lustre I have from the old store. I will make that into a low waist for dinner this week. It is a good thing I can sew!

We were out under the trees till a few minutes ago, when it began to rain. It is now half past six. There is no service at the Cathedral in the evening, only in the afternoon at three. This is an awkward hour for us as we have no time for dinner with it being a long way to St. Mary's from Sunville.

Cousin Frank will be home from school next week and the girls on the 27th. Phoebe says she wants me to stay with her till the end of August for all the holidays. There are many parties and social events planned.

Tuesday July 6th

It was dreadfully wet yesterday, so that there was no Tennis Tournament. Miss Aston and Ted came in for a few minutes last night and they said that they would begin the tennis at Sunville this morning. I have done up the flowers all over the house, roses in nine vases on the dining table. I made Moss cake and put part in patty pans. It looks nice. I always make the cake for Tuesdays when people come calling. Mrs. Tom and Mrs. Baylor are in Town, as Cousin Tom cannot come home for dinner today. We are to eat at two so as to get over early to the Tennis Club.

Yesterday I went over to see Aunt Sophia in the afternoon and found Mary up to her eyes in work. Mrs. Foot, Jack's sister and child, are coming today to Bracken Brae on a visit. On Sunday there was a letter from Uncle Ben to say he was better and would be coming down on Wednesday. As Mary has only one spare room, she had to do up the drawing room for Uncle (she has a big sitting room.) He will only stay a few days.

Thursday 8th

Tuesday we did not leave the Tennis Ground until seven, and then we were in such a hurry to dress as tea was at eight. Cousin Phoebe wore black satin with yellow silk and lace and looked lovely. I wore my black velvet skirt, white and black stockings, patent leather slippers, white muslin blouse, with the crimson plaid ribbon Aunt Emily gave me years ago and crimson roses on my shoulder in the front. I was told I looked very nice.

There were twenty-two of us at the side table. Ted took the

head and carved the ducks and I poured out the tea. We were very jolly, had a much better time than those at the big table. After tea we had music, cards, and billiards.

At supper, Mrs. Baylor said I made the cakes and told everyone she would recommend them, so they went down well. Mr. Fogarty and Mrs. Baylor agreed that I was a very nice, clever, useful girl. As they were each married, they, the Cleeves, and Jack Boyd made so many remarks that I was the colour of my rose. Ted asked me, "Emmie what colour is red?"

There is no use minding their chaff, as I only get more if I mind. There is a Mr. Kelly and Mr. Hare visiting. They tease me about Mr. Hare because he is big and they say we would make a fine pair. Then they tease me over Mr. Kelly because he has been in Canada and we have plenty to talk about. He is a Post Office Manager and is well off. He's got red hair, is very goody, though quite harmless. He says he plans to live in Canada when he is better off.

Wednesday we were in town in the morning, and on our way home I heard a bugle. It was the judge in a carriage and pair, footman and coachman, with ten mounted police in charge. Fancy needing so much protection! Old Ireland is still a bad place to live in.

In the afternoon, we were at the Tennis Club again. Kathleen won on the double, lost in the single. We hurried home to dress for the Fogarty's. We had a nice evening at Westburn where there were sixteen to dinner. We did not get home till twelve.

Today Phoebe and I went over to see Uncle Ben for tea at Bracken Brae. We then drove in to Town in the little Trap. I did some of the driving and shopping for Phoebe while she was being fitted for two silk blouses.

Then, in the rain, we sat for three hours again at the Tennis Club Tournament. In spite of the wet, I had a fine time. It was like playing in a bog and oh, but the players were muddy! The final is put off till Monday. Two of my friends won prizes.

I had a fine hot cup of tea at the Club, which warmed me up. Mr. Kelly got it for me. He was quite attentive, got me a dry seat etc. Oh, won't I catch it when I see Joe! He sat opposite us, and I knew he was trying to catch my eye, but I would not look at him.

Saturday 10th

Frank Cleeve has finished the school term in London and is home now. He is a jolly handsome fellow, well made. Mary Boyd says all girls fall in love with him. She says Ethel did and she warned me I might be next. But I have no fears of that. After all, I am two years older than Frank and three older than Ethel.

It cleared up at eleven yesterday and then the sun came out hot, so we went to the Dean's garden party. I was dressed as on Sunday, and two people told Cousin Phoebe I was a very nice looking girl. The green ribbon is becoming as my skin is clearer and I am getting fat, (but no pimples.) Uncle Ben says he sees a great change for the better. I look quite young, I am told.

Phoebe wore black satin with pale cornflower blue trimmings, lace and jet beads to match, satin sunshade lined with white lace and turned with blue ribbon. Of course she looked very handsome. We left here at four, returning at seven. There were about fifty people and I saw some lovely dresses. The grounds were nice and the flowers and vegetable gardens grand. I quite enjoyed myself.

There was tea, cake, bread and butter, strawberries and ice cream which is a rare thing here. Ice is hard to get.

I spent yesterday morning at Bracken. Mrs. Foot is very nice, very pretty, jolly and musical. (Father would have known her as Miss Susie Boyd when he lived here.) At nine last night, Tom and I went over to Beachlawn as usual on a Friday. Phoebe remained with Mrs. Baylor. "The Brackens" were there for tea and Miss Haddlsey, Mr. Hudson, and Mr. Morris, were there for the evening. Joe gives me no end of chaff when he sees me in the Billiards room with Frank. I moved to the music room to get away from him. It was after ten when we got home.

Your letter just came in. The thought of your being ill has made me feel dreadfully. You must let me know every time you write if you are better or I SHALL GO HOME! My hip is fine and I am well. Tell father I was pleased with his nice letter. It will do him good to go about with people. I will write to him next week. Send him my love and a kiss.

Ever darling Mother.

Your loving child,

Emily

Kathleen Cleeve Chides Her Husband Joe

Sympathetic towards her young cousin Emmie, Cousin Kathleen has decided to confront her husband, Joe Cleeve, over his constant teasing. Not that she would do so in front of the rest of the family, Kathleen waited until they were in the privacy of the bedroom to speak up. "I do think Joe that you ought to lay off poor Emmie! Can't you see that she is terribly shy when it comes to any attention she receives from the young men? Emmie is NOT a dance hall girl and does not deserve to be treated like one. For God's sake, Joe, give her some respect."

Somewhat taken aback, Joe defended himself. "I mean no harm, Kathleen. The girl needs to loosen up a little. She's far too serious and will scare the boys off. She should be thick-skinned enough to handle a little teasing."

Determined to set Joe straight, Kathleen retorted, "A little teasing?" You never let up on her, Joe. Between you, Tom and Ted, the girl doesn't get a moment's peace. How ever will love blossom if a gang of senseless louts makes her ashamed of her feelings? If you keep on this way, you'll sabotage the whole plan."

Unaccustomed to being challenged, Joe mounted a strong counter attack. "Senseless louts? Is that what you think of the Cleeve men? Do you think we got to be the most successful businessmen in the county by being senseless louts? And do you think you got to live at one of the most prestigious addresses in Limerick by being married to the village idiot?"

"I'm not saying you are feeble-minded," Kathleen replied with all the composure she could muster. "Just treat Emmie with the respect that a well-bred and modest young lady deserves. You can't go trampling all over the sensibilities of an innocent girl and have any good come of it. Besides, she is a guest in our homes. Emmie's parents have entrusted us with a sacred duty to find their only daughter a suitable mate for the rest of her life. They are counting on us to do right by her."

"Well. I was only trying to be helpful- to get her thinking about the joys of marital bliss. How's she going to pick out a husband if she doesn't even think about what a husband is for? If you ask me, the girl is rather clueless."

Kathleen became frustrated with her husband's truculence. "There's a difference between clueless and innocent! Though, I'm sure God knows that when he made men in the first place, they couldn't possibly know the meaning of the word 'innocent'. Leave this situation up to the ladies. We will dress her up so she's enticing to the right sort of young men. Her good character and sweetness will do all the rest. We don't need to be harassed with a barrage of lewd remarks from our men folk."

"Lewd? Lewd, my arse! I never used any bad language in the presence of the ladies!" Realizing he had just fallen into a trap, Joe decided he would not win this battle and prepared to accept defeat.

"You just did, Joe. And I'll thank you to put a stop to it this instant. I'll not share my bed with a man who has got the mouth of a sailor. You can just collect your pillow and blanket and spend the night in the Billiard room. Maybe a night on your own will help you see things in their proper light. Now get on with you, and Goodnight, Sir!"

Joe retrieved his pillow and a blanket and shuffled out the bedroom door, his shoulders stooped and gaze downcast. This was indeed a bitter pill to swallow. "Women!" he muttered. "I'll never understand them!"

~~~~

SEVEN

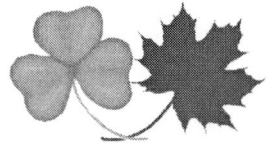

Plotting Behind The Scenes

Tom Cleeve Pays a Visit to His Mother Sophia

Mary Cleeve was tending the garden when her brother Tom sprinted up the path at Bracken Brae. She bid him a cheery good-morning and remarked, "We seldom see you here so early in the day, Tom. To what do we owe the pleasure of your company?"

Tom had obviously been in a hurry and responded with concern in his voice, "Mother called over to the house this morning and asked me to come by. Have you any idea what she wants? I hope she is not ill."

Mary wiped the soil from her hands on her apron as she sought to reassure her brother, "Oh no, Tom. Mother is fit as a fiddle. Have no fear. It is Emmie she is worried about."

"Emmie?" Tom queried, "What could be wrong with Emmie? I just saw her at breakfast and she looked quite fine to me. Pretty as a picture."

Mary waved Tom towards the door, "Mother is dressed and reading the morning paper in the drawing room. She'll fill you in on all there is to know."

Tom let himself in and found his mother sitting bolt upright in her chair. He strode across the room and brushed her forehead with a perfunctory kiss. "Good morning, Mother. I do hope you are keeping well."

"Yes Tom, it's lovely to see you," she replied with affection. "Thank you for coming on such short notice. I would not bother you under ordinary circumstances but there's a family matter I must speak with you about. I've heard some unsettling news and it's become rather urgent."

"Mary says you are concerned about Emmie. Have you had bad news from Canada?"

"I wouldn't call it bad news," Sophia hesitated, "...it's concerning all the same. As you know, we have a little family intrigue to pursue that takes the form of some matchmaking. Your sister Mary tells me that Emmie has confided that she is anxious to get back home to Canada."

"Back to Canada," Tom bristled, "Why she's only just arrived. I sent a cheque to cover her expenses for a proper visit. How could she possibly be thinking of going home so soon?"

Sensing Tom's annoyance, Sophia chose her words carefully, " It seems that Emmie plans to return to Dublin at the end of summer to stay with Ben and Mary for a few weeks. She insists she will then return to her mother in Canada as she worries that Bel must not spend the winter alone without Willie or the two older boys at home. I must say, Emmie is not to be faulted for putting the well being of her family first. We have all seen how she constantly sets herself aside for the benefit of others and this is a fine trait indeed. However, Bel has written, imploring us to do everything in our power to persuade Emmie to stay here in Ireland. She and Willie remain resolved that Emmie must find a husband."

"Well of course she must find a husband. That's what the girl is here for. She just needs to get on with it!"

Still choosing her words carefully, Sophia attempted to calm Tom's annoyance, "It is not Emmie's fault that she was unaware of her parents' plan. We all were quite certain that she would just fall in love. Now I need not explain to you son, that this situation sets the cat amongst the pigeons! We can hardly expect to promote the course of true love when the girl is on the fly to return home. She has not taken to any of the young men she has met thus far and perhaps that's all to the good."

"All to the good, Mother?" Tom quizzed, "What good is there in Emmie not warming up to someone? Haven't we introduced her to plenty of fine young men?"

Sophia chose her moment, "Well Tom, perhaps she hasn't been bitten by the love bug for the RIGHT young man. Oh Tom, I had so hoped that there might be a match between your Frank and Emmie! They appear to have got off to a good start since he returned from school. A family alliance would be grand. Emmie is a Journeaux on her mother's side, just as I am a Journeaux. We know she comes from good stock and that goes a long way. Not to mention that I have not met any young woman in Limerick who can match her abilities in managing a home. It is indeed remarkable!"

"Well you're right about that," Tom conceded. "Have I not remarked on many occasions that Emmie would make a fine wife? But Frank has only been home from school a few weeks....there hasn't been enough time to establish a proper courtship."

Pleased that Tom had altered his focus to Frank, Sophia

captured the moment, "Well perhaps there is not time to dawdle. My point is that it goes both ways. Emmie would benefit from marrying into the Cleeve family just as much as Frank would benefit from having her as his wife. You know better than any how important it is for a man with large responsibilities to have a good mate. I fear that we may miss the opportunity as Emmie seems so insistent to get home."

"I don't know where I'd be without dear Phoebe." Tom softened, "Your point is well taken, Mother. None of the local girls can hold a candle to Emmie's abilities. Why, she could run Sunville with her hands tied behind her back. Phoebe is so impressed with Emmie. And one day, Frank will be the master of Sunville...."

Sophia was well pleased that the conversation was exactly where she wanted it to be. "Do you think you could have a word with Frank and see where he stands? I would not normally interfere but it seems that time is now of the essence. Frank is fond of the ladies and I dare say a man can fall in love with one woman as easily as the next. He might as well set his sights in the best direction and choose a fine woman who will serve him well over the long term."

"That's absolutely right Mother, " Tom agreed, "There's no time to lose. But if she's intent on returning to Canada, how can Emmie be persuaded to stay?"

Sophia produced an heirloom emerald ring from a small silver box on her side table, "Perhaps if Emmie were formally engaged it would distract her from thoughts of returning to Canada. There's no telling how a real commitment might change her view of things. If Frank is willing, I'd like to offer him my emerald ring to put on his young lady's finger. Your father gave it to me many years ago and it is a lovely one indeed."

"May he rest in peace," Tom mused. "Yes, father would be ever so pleased to see that ring on the finger of his grandson's bride. That's very generous of you, Mother. I will pass your offer on to Frank. And now I must be off to the office. There are plenty of business engagements to keep me occupied there."

Tom kissed his mother's forehead once again as he raised from his chair. Sophia walked to the door with her son, adding a final word of caution, " Please see what you can do before too long Tom. I fear we will miss the boat if some action behind the scenes is not taken to help these two young people along. We do not want to miss a fine opportunity."

As Tom headed out the door, obviously engrossed in thoughts of his business, he assured his mother, "Yes mother, I will see to it directly. In the mean time, there are business opportunities at Cleeve Brothers that must not be missed. I must get a move on."

Emmie Writes to Her Brother Ben

Sunville House

July 18th 1897

My Darling Brother Ben,

I was very pleased to get your letter telling me about the nice time you had in Montreal at the Jubilee Celebrations. It will be something to remember all your life. Too bad Mother was not able to go. I hope you help Mother all you can. We must take good care of her.

The Regatta here is over. It was a success in spite of a wet day. It was a holiday in Limerick so everyone turned out to see it as thousands of people lined the riverbanks. The Sunvilles, Beechlawns, and Brackens, with a party, all making 25, boarded the Yacht close to here at half past three and we followed all the race boats up and down.

At five we had tea and cake, the Sunville maids being on board. Then when the Regatta was over, we had supper in two lots, as the Saloon would not hold all at once. It is a lovely little yacht with three cabins, holding six people for a night, but the deck is big enough for 30 or 40.

After the Regatta we moored to the dock to watch the fireworks which were very good. A man came down from Dublin to show them off. I never saw better. It was near twelve when we got home.

Thursday Morning.

We were out of town today paying some visits and every field we passed had haymakers at work. I wish you could see them work. It is like child's play. They stop to look, stop to talk, stop to light a pipe; indeed the workers are a lazy lot. It has been hot today and when we were in town, everyone seemed to be so lazy, the shop men were slow, indeed the town only seemed half awake.

When we got back home it was just three, our dinner hour, so I drove in to the factory for Cousin Tom and brought him back. He does not like driving himself. I find it hard to remember to keep to my left, and with crowds of donkeys, it is quite hard to get along on William Street.

Before I went in to town at about twelve, I went over to see Aunt Sophia for a few minutes. She expects to see me every day or two. Cousin Dawse and Ruth will come over to stay with her on the 8th of August. Aunt is quite excited about it.

Her garden is grand. I wish you boys could get the kinds of fruit I get. I am full to the brim with strawberries, raspberries and gooseberries. I have been helping Cousin Phoebe to hull strawberries. This is the third lot of jam she has made. My cakes are as much appreciated here as by my young brothers at home. I am to make a big one on Saturday for the girls who are expected Tuesday 27th, my Birthday.

Cousin Joe and Kathleen are going to London next week. Young Olive and I are great friends. I think she is fond of me. Aylmer, her brother, is so deaf it is quite sad. The doctor is treating him. He is plain but Charley is a nice looking little boy. Vera is so old fashioned. She says some very funny things. She is plain but baby is very pretty.

Friday morning

I played Tennis with Frank yesterday at the Fogarty's, Uncle Ben's old home. Then we went to Beechlawn for tea in a big tent. Olive and Miss Haddlsey were also there. What a jolly tea we had and the table looked lovely. It was laden with chicken, ham, sardines, peaches, pie, melon, green plumbs, chocolates, white and brown bread and toast. Today there is tennis at Beechlawn. I hope to play again.

Have you cut the Tennis court since Dick left home? I hope you boys do not let Mother go up and down cellar. You must be sure to help her well, especially in the garden. Have you any sweet peas yet?

I must stop now. Give my love to Harry and tell him to write to me.

Ever Dear Ben,

Your loving sister,

      Emmie

Tom Cleeve Has a Heart to Heart Talk with Frank

Frank Cleeve had just entered the front hallway of Sunville with tennis racquet in hand and with a soggy Turkish towel around his neck. The house seemed unusually quiet and, thinking he was alone, Frank called out, "Anybody home?"

Tom Cleeve poked his head out of the study doorway, "Ah, there you are Frank. How was the tennis?"

"Emmie gave me a good run for my money over at Beechlawn just now. I'm drenched with sweat and parched!"

"Well do come into the study and have a drink with me. How about a whiskey and soda? I've some business to discuss with you, son."

Unbuttoning his shirt, Frank replied, "Thanks Father, but can't it wait? I'm in dreadful need of a bath and dry clothes."

"I'm sure your bath can wait, Frank." Tom poured whiskey into two Waterford crystal glasses and spritzed them with soda from a silver and glass dispenser. "Please close the door and have a seat."

"Very well, Father." Frank sensed that his father had something important to say as he accepted the glass that his father handed him. "What's on your mind?"

"Well Frank, when I go over to London in August, I'd like you to come with me. It's about time you started to get a feel for things in the London operation of the business. There are some people I'd like you to meet and they need to get to know you. Once you have completed your studies, you will be taking on a significant role in Cleeve Brothers and I want my people in England to get accustomed to seeing you at the helm, so to speak."

"Capital!" Frank exclaimed. "That would be grand. Of course I'd be happy to meet your business associates and get a feel for the London side of things. I hadn't expected to have the opportunity till next year."

Gauging that Frank was in an affable mood, Tom pressed on. "I so look forward to having you on board, Frank, and it warms my heart to know that my first-born will one day take over the business entirely. Mind you, I'm certain that your old man still has a few good years left in him, but all the same, I'd rest easier if I knew my successor was learning the ropes.

Your uncle Joe will help you. He is the clever one and will give you an excellent training on the job. Fred can see that you know the ins and outs of the factory here in Limerick. Ted will show you the 'country-side' of things in Mallow and Knocklong. You can expect to work hard and put in long hours. But when you see the success that comes of your efforts, you will be well satisfied."

"Oh yes, father. I am so looking forward to traveling and seeing more of the world. It will be wonderful to broaden my horizons and get more acquainted with the business at the same time."

Perturbed that Frank had taken the conversation in a different direction, Tom searched for a way to get back on track. "Yes, all that is true, son, but I have to say that of all the grand times I've had over the years, nothing beats returning to hearth and home at the end of the day. It is such a wonderful feeling for a man to come home at night to his wife and family and see just what it is he toils so hard for. You and your mother and brother and sisters are my reason for being. Without your dear mother, I wouldn't be half the success that I've become. What they say about a good woman being behind every successful man is entirely true."

"Well, I wouldn't know anything about that," Frank chortled. "I quite enjoy playing the field and being footloose and fancy-free. Surely you can remember the days when you were young and in your prime?"

"Well son, that brings me to something I've been wanting to ask you." Tom rubbed his chin as he searched for words, "It's a delicate matter, but a very important one Frank. I was wondering if you'd given any thought to settling down? I mean with a good woman. I know you've enjoyed playing the field and building a reputation for being somewhat of a ladies man. And that's all to the good. It never does any harm for a man to know he's well appreciated by the fairer sex...."

Frank interrupted, raising his glass, "I'll drink to that Father!"

Tom continued gingerly, "There comes a time, however, when one would do well to think about the future. Think, for example, about your dear mother and how she has created such a wonderful home here at Sunville for us. Think what life might be like without her....not that your mother isn't in robust health mind you. But my point is that a successful man needs a good woman at his side, someone to come home to at night and ease the cares of the day."

"Yes Father," Frank agreed. "I could not have asked for a better mother than the woman you chose to fill that role in my life. But what does Mother have to do with the role I will be taking on in the family business?"

Tom had become decidedly uncomfortable as he realized that Frank was not following his thread, "Well son, a good wife is just as important as the right education, training and business opportunity. If I were you, Frank, I wouldn't wait too long to set your sights on a woman who fits the bill for you over the long term. Not simply someone that happens to get the juices going, if you get my drift, but someone who can manage your home as well as you would manage your business."

Frank looked rather non-plussed and asked, "What are you getting at Father?"

"I'm talking about marriage," Tom blurted out, "Marriage with the right sort of girl. For example, there happens to be a gem right under our very roof these days. I'm speaking of course, about your cousin Emmie. I cannot say when I have ever met so capable and accomplished a young woman! She can do just about anything and SHE DOES! She is cheerful and willing and extremely generous. And she is certainly not hard to look at either. All the Cleeve men say they would be proud to walk down the street with Miss Woodburn on their arm."

"Good Lord, Father. I dare say Emmie IS a good-looking girl. But I hadn't been thinking in the slightest about marriage. Not now! I will be returning to school in the Fall to complete my final year. How could I manage to be a husband and a scholar at the same time? Isn't this just a little premature?"

Tom squirmed in his leather chair as he gulped down the

remainder of his drink. "Well son, I'm sure you have a point. But I'm also certain that Emmie will not be available for long. One thing I've learned in the business world is to strike when the opportunity presents itself. If you drag your feet, you'll miss out. The same applies to selecting a mate. Of course, if you just don't care for Emmie..."

Frank shot back, "I think I see where this is going. I must say that I do indeed admire my cousin. She is ever so accomplished but a trifle too serious. As a matter of fact, I've made it my mission to lighten her up. If you think I ought to take her more seriously, Father, I'm up for the challenge."

Somewhat relieved, Tom added, " I wouldn't presume to push the matter, but you might want to think about the long haul. If you find that there are any warm feelings in your heart for Emmie, I'd advise you to cultivate them. It seems she is talking of returning to Canada much sooner than we expected and I fear she may slip through our fingers."

Feeling somewhat pressured, Frank stammered, "What?...were you thinking of a marriage this summer?"

"Oh no son, there's no rush to get married. But if I were you, I'd be thinking about your future. You don't want to be kicking yourself that you let a fine woman get away. A long engagement is quite acceptable and if you need to sew a few wild oats in the mean time, there's ample opportunity to do so when you are away at school. For the time being, if you are so disposed, you might bring up the topic with Emmie and see how she responds."

"I think I get your drift, father. One doesn't become engaged with thoughts of wiggling out of the arrangement, so it would do well to broach the subject to find out if Emmie has any interest at all. If she does, I suppose I could handle a long engagement while getting used to the idea of settling down. What would Emmie do while I am finishing school?"

"Oh, no trouble there, Frank. Emmie would be such a help to your mother. It can get lonely here at Sunville with me working such long hours and you children away at school. Joe and Kathleen would like her to stay with them for a while. She is such a help with the children. She has also mentioned going to visit the Butlers at Wilton. And of course, she is expected to spend some time with Uncle Ben and Aunt Mary in Dublin."

"Well I guess that takes care of the next twelve months," Frank calculated. "I must confess that Mother and Grandmother are extremely fond of Emmie and that says a lot to recommend her. As a matter of fact, the whole family appears to have welcomed her with open arms....even young Cecil- who can be such a pain."

Feeling very satisfied that the conversation had gone well, Tom decided he had only one final piece of advice to impart. "I'm asking you to give the matter some thought soon, Frank. If you put it off, it may end up being too late. I want the best for you in all ways. And if you decide to pursue the matter, be sure to be a gentleman in ALL WAYS. Emmie is on the shy side and it may take some chasing to catch her. But that's all to the good. You wouldn't want the prize to come too easy...there's no satisfaction in that!"

"Of course, Father. I'll mind my P's and Q's. Now, I really must have that bath. Was there anything else?"

"No son, that was it. Off you go. And you may help yourself to some of that cologne in my bathroom. You really do smell quite dreadful. That does not go over well with the ladies at all and...." Tom left his sentence to trail off as Frank disappeared out the study door. He was well pleased with himself and made a mental note to report to Sophia that he had done his part.

Birthday Greetings

Sunville House

July 25th 1897

My Darling Mother,

Very very many happy returns of this day. I hope your next birthday will find more of the family home to visit. I suppose, with four sons we are not likely to be all living together, but please God that you mother, dear father, and I will be together. You have not been often out of my thoughts today.

Phoebe and I are alone just now; we went to church in the morning and read all afternoon. Ted came in at five and remained for tea. He has just left for Bracken where he will find the family gathered. We did not go as the maids were out and the day has been very wet and windy.

We drove in to Town yesterday and saw Cousin Tom and Miss Aston off by the four o'clock train. She lives in Birmingham so they part at Liverpool. She was sorry to say good-bye to Limerick.

I posted my home letters while in town. Ethel wrote to Beechlawn last week from the Jeffrey's and said her mother was coming out to keep house for Lord Aylmer while Lalla was in London. What has become of Paget and Gerald Aylmer while Isabella is away?

Cousin Phoebe says the white blouse I made fits like a dressmaker's cut, which is nice- and she is particular! She sees that this house is kept beautifully, never a spot. Mind you, there is too much brushing and cleaning, I think, for I do not do anything to clean up these days. The silver is polished every day and the glass and plate rubbed with a shammy by the maid before being put on the table.

It is after eleven, so I must stop, but it was late before Ted left, and I have been wanting to write you a line today. Good night darling little woman.

July 27th, Tuesday.

Darling Mother, this morning at Breakfast your loving letters came. It was so nice to get them on the very day of my birthday and what a relief it was to hear Dear Father had work, even if the pay is only small. It is well that he got something.

Now dear Mother, as Father will not be home, of a certainty I will go home for Christmas. I will not leave you alone all the long winter. If we move in to Montreal in the Spring, it would be best for us to have the few months to get ready slowly. I will then have been seven months away, quite long enough.

And now it is ten o'clock and we are off to town. A telegram has just arrived to say the mail train broke down, so Eileen and Lil cannot get home till two. Frank is to play in the Tennis Tournament at three with Kathleen, so there is not much time to have lunch. We will all go over to see the match. The Fogartys will come back with us for dinner and then we all go to a Band Concert, so goodbye till tomorrow.

Frank has just come in with the most beautiful bouquet of

white roses for my birthday. He had them sent up from town with a little card that said, "From your admiring cousin with great affection, Frank." He is a sweet boy but ought not to be spending money unnecessarily. I dare say all are making far too great a fuss over me.

Wednesday 28th

We waited for an hour and a half at the station as the train was very late. To pass the time, Frank and I walked up the railway line about a quarter of a mile to a stand where the tickets are taken and watched the poor mad people just opposite the lunatic Asylum. Then when the train came in, we got into the carriage with the young people.

Eileen is short and very quick and sharp with her tongue. She has pretty hair and bright complexion- is quite nice looking. But Lillie is very pretty, almost as tall as me, with lovely hair, pretty hands, bright red lips and good colour. She will be a lovely woman. They have lovely things, both to wear and for ornaments. They are petted children of rich parents. They are very nice to me.

It was very wet all afternoon yesterday. We went over to see the tennis but it was too wet to go to the Band. The Fogartys and Mr. Wilson who is staying with them had dinner with us and the Beechlawns came in the evening. The girls went off to bed at nine as they were very tired from traveling all the night before. Frank helped me with the supper and we locked up the house together.

The last three nights since Tom left, Phoebe and I have gone around with a candle and tried all the doors and windows. Frank has just now gone into town and the girls are shopping for hats and dresses with their mother. The girls are going over to see Aunt

Sofia in a little although it is raining hard. I do not think they will be able to go to see the sports if this rain continues.

I am just as well pleased as I do not feel up for much. My hip is not well today. I thought I would write to Aunt Mary Journeaux as I am alone. I will tell her that I cannot stay in Ireland all Winter and so will not be up for the horse show. Phoebe says I must stay here in August.

Friday 30th

Darling Mother, I did not write yesterday as I was out all day. For Wednesday, in spite of the rain, we all went to the sports. They were the same as those I saw in June. I wore black skirt, print blouse, and my cape, so I did not mind the rain. We got home at eight and had a hot dinner. We dine in style now at half past eleven. Yesterday I told the girls to do up the flowers, but they would not and indeed, will not do any of my little jobs. They are spoiled indeed.

We went to bed at eleven last night and Lil and I had a pillow fight before we slept. I had a bad night with toothache and must go to a dentist as the filling has come out of two teeth. I dread to think what that will cost me.

Cousin Phoebe went off at ten in the trap with Frank to meet Tom at the station. (He has been in London.) Eileen and Lil went out for a ride, so I did up my flowers and pressed a skirt for Eileen. Then I went over to Bracken Brae to collect Lil. We all dressed for lunch, then went over to the Tennis Club to see Frank and Kathleen play. They were beaten. It was after eleven when we got in and had dinner.

Tom went over to see Aunt Sophia on a matter of family

business, he said. Fred, Olive and Joe came over here. I am doing some crochet for Phoebe. She wants me to do her enough for a bedroom set in yellow for her room. It is spool linen and will be a long job. I don't know how I will finish it before I return to Canada.

It is ten now and we have just finished breakfast. The three young people have gone for a ride, Tom to his office, and Phoebe is about the house. I promised Kathleen yesterday to go over this morning and help her do some sewing for the children. I am also to make some doll dresses for Vera. Kathleen is doing an awful lot and is tired, trying to get off to England on Wednesday.

The telephone just rang. Kathleen was speaking, asking us all over there for tea. Mary is here and says she dreads Dawse and Ruth's visit. She calls them the Duke and Duchess as they are so grand. They say Cousin Jennie is much better now. She is taking swell singing lessons in Dublin and will be home next week.

Monday the first of August is a holiday here. If the weather is fine, we are all to go out in the yacht for the day - only ourselves, the Beechlawns, and Fernbanks. It will be nicer than a large crowd. We will take dinner and tea with us, as we will be out all day.

The girls will not do anything but admire themselves. They even will not get the supper, so I make Frank help me. He is most willing. We fight and lecture each other like cousins. Seeing them all being petted and kissed makes me feel homesick. I want my mother to coddle me. I have no one here although all are very kind. I am afraid I would not like being coddled by any but my own people, for I hate being mauled as you know. I am too independent!

I meant to have written to Edward, but as I am sending Aunt's letter, I must wait. Please give all the boys my love. I will write to some of them next week. Thank them all for their letters and tell Dear Father how thankful I am he has work, and pray God it will bring something better. I must stop now and will finish this tomorrow.

Saturday 31st

We had tea at nine at Beechlawn last night, after being from four until eight at the Lewis' for tennis. Aunt Sophia and Mrs. Fogarty won ladies doubles, and Miss Haddlsey ladies singles. Frank won men's singles. Now the Tournament is over.

I helped Kathleen for two hours yesterday with her sewing. They asked me to spend a month with them after they come home from England, but I refused, as I must stay two months in Dublin before I return to Canada. We had a nice tea and lots of fun. I sat between Frank and Lil and fought with Frank all the time under the table.

After tea, we young people and Joe played hide and seek until dark. Then Frank and I went off for a long stroll. When we came in they had finished supper and, of course, all wanted to know where we had been and what we were up to. It was twelve when we came in.

It is dreadfully hot today as it was yesterday. I have not much clothes on. Lil and I have had a game of tennis and I have had a bath and changed my clothes as I was so wet when I sat down to write. Eileen is at the dentist today. Frank is going to take me to have my teeth filled (they are very bad) on Tuesday. He has gone up to the Junction to meet Cecil, who comes home at 1:25.

Frank is very kind to the girls and so good to his mother. They are all proud of her. She is so fine looking. I think Lil is the pet. I like her the best of the two girls, perhaps because I know her best as we sleep together. Please give my love to all who ask for me. I will write to Ethel in a few days.

With much love to all. Ever Dear Little Mother.

Your loving child,

Emmie

Frank Recounts the Details of the Evening to his Parents

Frank Cleeve just wasn't accustomed to being rebuffed by the ladies. After returning to Sunville late at night, he found his parents in the downstairs sitting room. Both Tom and Phoebe had an expectant look on their faces. "Well Frank...?"

"Well..... my dear mother and father, it didn't go the way I had expected. I just don't know what to make of my Canadian Cousin. Perhaps all the ladies in Canada behave as she does, or else Emmie is out of her mind. She seems to have not the slightest idea that she is here to get married."

Tom rolled his eyes and threw his hands up in the air. "I knew it was a bad idea to send her here without discussing the purpose of her visit. How can we be expected..."

Phoebe reached out and grasped Tom's arm, shushing him to allow Frank to continue.

Frank remained incredulous. "As you know, Emmie and I went off on a stroll along the North Circular Road. The warm air was ever so lovely and the twilight made for a terribly romantic atmosphere. Emmie was rather distressed though. She was babbling on about her family at home and how worried she is about them.

I told her not to be silly. Things have turned around for them as her father and both Eddie and Dick have got work now. Her mother only has the two young boys to look after now so much of her responsibilities have been lifted. The boys will be able to return to school in the Fall as there are now three incomes to take care of the bills.

But Emmie would hear none of it. And what a time I had trying to steer her to another topic of conversation! I told Emmie that she was being far too serious and that she needs to set aside her cares - to let herself be looked after by a strong admiring man.

Thinking it would do well to pay her some compliments, I took her hand in a comforting sort of way. I told her, "Emmie, you are one of the loveliest girls I have ever met. You have so many talents and abilities that I cannot help but deeply admire you. Father and Mother cannot say enough to praise you and I agree wholeheartedly. As a matter of fact, despite knowing you for only a short time, I am quite smitten. I do pray that you would consent to our becoming engaged to be married."

Well then didn't she pull her hand away and turn red in the face. She could barely keep her composure as she stammered, "No Frank...I must go home to my family in Canada. I am most taken aback by this. I had not the slightest idea you were thinking of marriage. You must not take my refusal personally. It's just that I don't want to marry anyone. Your place is here in Ireland with the family business. I long to return to my home in Canada. Mother and Father have need of me there."

I couldn't believe my ears so just blurted it out, "Emmie, how could you be so naïve? You must be some sort of ninny not to realize that the whole purpose of your visit is to find a husband. Your family is financially ruined with the loss of the business. If they cannot even afford to send your brothers to school, what makes you think they can afford to keep you? What's more, you could not do better than to marry into the Cleeve family. We will keep you in fine style and there will be nothing to worry that pretty head of yours. I am most certain that it would be a great relief to your parents to see you well looked after."

Tom could no longer contain himself. "How dare she! This is just preposterous! Emmie needs to be taught her place. Doesn't she realize...."

Phoebe interrupted. "Now Tom. Calm down. This is only the beginning of the game. Emmie has been well brought up. Of course she isn't going to jump at the first offer that presents itself. She is playing hard-to-get. And so she should! The two of you make it sound as though all is lost. I assure you, it is not so! Frank just needs to stay the course. Emmie will come round."

"She's being stubborn," Tom insisted.

Phoebe came to the rescue. "Just because you didn't get your way on the first try, does not mean there is anything wrong with Emmie. She is a virtuous young lady. And you DO want to be assured of marrying a woman of virtue Frank, if you understand my deeper meaning. For the time being, leave this matter up to the Cleeve women. Mary and Mother Cleeve will give her wise counsel. The hour is late and I suggest we put this matter to rest for tonight. We could all do with some sleep."

"All the same," Tom grumbled, I don't like it."

Phoebe cut her husband off and kissed Frank on the cheek. "I am well pleased with you, son. You have done very well by taking the first step. Do not think that this is the end of it by any means. I suggest we all just carry on as though nothing has happened. A woman's feelings are delicate and Emmie just needs some time and space to adjust. I am certain she will come round!"

Tom and Frank shuffled out of the sitting room and made their way up the grand staircase towards the bedrooms. According to her usual custom, Phoebe checked the latches on the doors and windows. Alone with her thoughts, she was not so certain about Emmie as she had made out to her men folk. Her intuition told her that something was amiss.

~~~~~

EIGHT

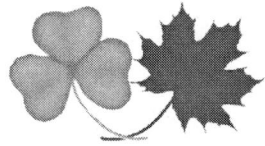

Emmie Longs To Go Home

Emmie Writes to Her Father About Finances

Sunville House

August 1st 1897

My Dear Father,

Thanks for your nice long letter. It was good of you to write to me from St. Hyacinth. I do so love to get home letters, and dear Dad, I am so pleased you have work. Even if the pay is not all it might be, it may lead to better. If we were together –and I pray that will be soon- if Edward and Dick boarded with us we could live on $600 if we were economical, which dear Mother is. Soon Harry will be earning, and then there will be only three of us to look after.

I do miss you and Mother so! I wonder if you think of me more on Sunday than on other days; for I never seem to forget you all that day, even for a moment. I do so hope you can be home with Mother today. I think you will see a change in me. Everyone says I look younger and my face is quite fat but not my body yet. How is Mother looking? Is she able to get along alone? You know I can go home any time I am needed.

This is Sunday morning and I have just dressed while the others are bathing etc. I am always the first, and such a row as there is for the bathroom. Uncle Ben came home last night and he is wild, indeed. The house has not one quiet moment.

Yesterday we all played a lot of tennis. The day was hot and we all had three baths. In the evening, the four young people here and the Fernbanks went off for a long Bike ride. I should like to be able to ride and Frank says he will teach me this week.

The Miss Kings come on Thursday, Dawse and Ruth on Saturday. The Beechlawns will go to England on Wednesday. I am very sorry as it would have been nice to have all the Cleeves together here. I am very fond of Joe and Kathleen. Kathleen is so very nice to me. Jennie Cleeve returned home from Dublin this week. I have not got to know her so well.

There is the gong for breakfast, so I must run.

Tom Cleeve Argues With His Sister Mary

Mary Cleeve has learned from Phoebe that Tom is in a state over Emmie's recent behaviour. Worried that he will make matters worse, she has gone into town to speak with him at the offices of Cleeve Brothers. The secretary has shown her into the inner office where Tom was to be found pouring over a stack of papers on his desk.

"Good morning, Tom dearest. It looks like business is thriving!"

"Don't Tom dearest me, sister! I know you have some lecture up your sleeve. You wouldn't come to visit me at the office without some ulterior motive."

"Now Tom," Mary replied. "Do be civil! I've come to talk to you about Frank and Emmie."

"Well I have something to say to you about Frank and Emmie." Tom countered. "Frank has gone out of his way to treat her well and to express his admiration. Now look at how she has repaid him! I'll not stand for it!"

Mary sat back in her chair and asked rather innocently, "Not stand for what Tom?"

Believing that he had the floor, Tom pleaded, "Mary, you've got to talk some sense into the girl's head. I knew that no good would come of sending her to Ireland without telling her the purpose of her visit. That was a mistake on the part of Willie and Bel. We cannot be expected to do our part in this matter if Emmie does not do hers. Frank has offered a proposal of marriage and Emmie has had the gall to turn him down!"

"Now Tom, calm down, " Mary chided. "It is not Emmie's fault if she has been kept in the dark. Not only that, she has been properly brought up and is innocent. She just needs some time to get used to the idea. Emmie is just a little shy…"

"Shy, fiddlesticks!" Tom blustered. "The girl is stubborn and defiant, that's what she is. It's a daughter's duty to obey her parents and that's all there is to it. I will not put up with a young woman going against the grain under my roof. She needs to remember her place!"

Mary came to Emmie's defense, "Tom, do ease up on her. How could Emmie 'obey' if she did not know what her Father required in the first place? You cannot fault her for...."

"Well, she knows now," Tom interrupted. "Frank has told her. Can you imagine? –turning down a proposal of marriage from Frank Cleeve! What is the girl thinking. Half the ladies of Limerick would give their eyeteeth to be engaged to Frank."

Mary knew she needed to placate her brother while remaining in charge at the same time. "I am sure she will come round, Tom. Emmie just needs a little time to get used to the idea. She and Frank have been getting on like a house on fire so far. Frank has indeed been most attentive and he and Emmie would be a fine match! You have to admit, it's only been a short while since he returned to Limerick. Believe me when I say that all is not lost.

Leave it up to me to talk to her, Tom. This is a time when a young woman needs her mother. Bel and I have been bosom pals since we were children. I will do my best to take Bel's place and give Emmie wise counsel. Mother will have a word too. Emmie is so respectful of her elders. She will listen to Mother's advice."

Tom mounted his rebuttal, "You women are a bunch of softies. The girl doesn't need to be molly coddled. She needs to be guided with a firm hand. She needs it made clear to her that it is the man who pays the piper that calls the tune. Emmie is in no position to call the shots. She is a woman – and penniless at that. If you ladies can't set her straight, I most certainly will."

Certain that Emmie would respond to a more gentle approach, Mary held her ground. "Mother and I will speak to her, Tom. Leave the matter in our hands. I am sure it will not come down to having to take a hard line approach. If we can avoid unpleasantness, that is all to the good. Besides, you have far more important business to deal with here at Cleeve Brothers. This is 'women's business' and you are better off leaving it to the women."

Tom was very fond of Emmie and realized then that he would rather not have to lay down the law. Perhaps Mary was right. "Very well, Mary. I will leave the matter with you and Mother. But mind you do not let her play you. Birds that won't sing have got to be made to sing. That's all there is to it."

Mary well knew that it was best to let her brother think he had had the last word. Sensing that his attention had returned to the pile of papers on his desk, Mary took her leave with a cheery, "Do have a wonderful day, Tom. I am so proud of how successful my brothers have become. Mother sends her regards too."

Emmie Gives the Appearance of Cheerfulness

Wednesday morning.

The last two days have flown by and I could not get a minute to write. On Sunday we all went to church, and after dinner, sat out under the trees with books until tea. Just before tea, Frank and I took a short walk and went up to Beechlawn for a while. It was too hot to go far. After tea we all went to Bracken, walking in a long line, taking up road and path. All the Cleeves were there, so Mary's room was full.

On Monday we had such a happy day, from nine in the morning till nine at night, we were on the yacht with two servants to do all the work. There was just ourselves, Olive and Ted. Kathleen was too busy to come and Miss Haddlsey is always seasick. Joe and Fred could not leave work.

The day was hot, but little sun. We went down to the mouth of the Shannon, almost into the mighty ocean. I learned to steer. Ted brought a gun but did not kill anything. Oh Dad, is not the river lovely? And some of the Grand Houses are lovely! Lord Emly's was the first as we went down but indeed, the least interesting.

The big house near Kilrush where the Reeves live is almost the nicest, although the Earl of Fitzgerald's estate is a grand old spot. He is to marry the Lord Dunraven's youngest daughter. She has plenty of money and is very good but he is poor. The Duke and Duchess of York will come down to the wedding about the twentieth of this month. Lord Dunraven lives at Adare and the mansion is now being done up for the Royal visitors. As they pass through Limerick, we hope to see them.

The naval review fleet is coming up to Cork to welcome the Duke and Duchess to Ireland. I wish the Cleeves would take the Yacht down to Cork for that. Next week we are to go to Kilkee for a day or two in the yacht, as the Miss Kings will be here. We are all burnt from being on the river. I had to wear green ribbons last night as my face was so red.

There was tennis here yesterday. I did the flowers with Lil and then cooked till dinner, took a bath as I was hot and changed my clothes. There were a good many here. All the Cleeve's and four others remained for tea. All left early as everyone seemed a bit out of sorts. It was not so jolly an evening as usual.

The gong went so I had to run and after breakfast, I drove in to Town with Tom to go to the dentist. Frank came on his wheel and took me to Mr. O'Megan who said I had four bad holes. I have to go again on Saturday and then in a fortnight when he hopes a nerve will be killed. I have a temporary stuffing in now. This will cost me a lot of money.

When I left Mr. O'Megan, Frank got into the chair. I meant to walk home, but met Mary at J.P. Evan's and she drove me to Beechlawn. We ran in there to see them as they leave for England at four today. I met Miss Haddlsey and several others. She asked us all to go down to Fernbank for tennis this afternoon and Mary invited the four young people over for tea, so Tom and Phoebe will be alone.

Friday morning

We had tennis at Fernbank on Wednesday and a jolly tea at Bracken Brae after, and yesterday tennis at the club. Phoebe and I went for a long walk; Tom and the young people for a bike ride. Phoebe is so kind to me. But I do miss my own dear Mother.

I had a letter from Miss Nancy Butler, written by Mr. Mather, asking me to go to them at Wilton Thursday 12th, as the house will be full in September. They thought I would go up to Dublin for the Horse Show and could stop there on my way. I have written to say no, as I do not want to leave here till the first of September, and it is too expensive. It would be over five pounds to go there and back, so I fear I shall not see Wilton.

I have just had a lovely long letter from Edward, also one from Dick. Dick says he wishes I would write to him, as when Mother sends on letters, they are stale, so I will send him one next week. It is nice Edward is seeing so much of the country. He seemed to have a nice time in Toronto Saturday and Sunday which must have done him good.

I do wish, my own dear Father, that you could be here with me and show me all your old haunts. I do so love Limerick and the Shannon, and much as I long to be with you all, shall be oh so sorry to say goodbye here. Of course, without my Canadian friends and family I could not be happy. I long to be home with you all.

I have such a lovely bunch of Jasmine and sweet lavender in my belt. It smells up the room. I wish you could get a sniff. We are to go to Kilkee on Thursday or Friday next for a few days. We will bathe in the sea, which will be lovely.

The young people ride here so much. I feel quite envious when I see them all go off together, but Cousin Phoebe is very good about walking with me so that I will not be lonely. Cecil is fond of me but he is a bold boy. However, he minds what I say to him and is often kissing and hugging me, which is not the way he treats his sisters. I find brothers never mind the sisters, but Frank makes him behave well, the only one who does.

Good night my dear Dad. Ever your own most loving child.

Emily Woodburn

Sunville House

August 5th 1897

My Darling little Mother,

I suppose I must write to you as well as to Father or you would be offended. Eileen and I are visiting together. All the family are in Town (it is near two). I have only just come in. Lil and I drove in to Town with Tom after breakfast. We did some shopping and I took some lovely mauve silk and lace to the dressmakers to get a blouse made. Cousin Phoebe gave me the silk yesterday for a birthday gift. I was very glad as I needed a pretty blouse. My white muslin is almost finished. I do it up every week, Cook washes it Mondays and I iron it on Tuesdays.

We were finished shopping at half past ten. I met Frank at the factory gate at eleven and he took me on a tour all over it. It was most interesting, but very hot and smelly. I should hate to work in it and feel sure Edward could not live in it. He is better off where he is, I think.

Frank rode into Town after, (at half past twelve) and we went in to Fernbank, which is close to the Factory. I had a chat with Miss Haddlsey and Olive. Ethel and Miss Haddlsey were great friends. She will tell you about her. I did not stay long, as they were going in to Town. Jennie comes home at seven tomorrow evening.

Eileen and I are talking so hard that we will not write very much. Phoebe says Ted is mean not to have given me a good present when he is so rich, but perhaps he will before I go. Did you ever ask Father if the cheque I came over on was from J.P. Evans or Cleeve Brothers? Tom keeps asking.

Mary and Sophia Discuss Strategy

Mary and Sophia were in the kitchen at Bracken Brae washing up the breakfast dishes. It was the maid's half day off. Sophia had been unusually quiet over the past few days but finally broke her silence, "Mary, when Emmie comes to visit tomorrow, we will have a chat with her. Please see to it that she comes alone as I do not want the other young people to interfere. It is best that you and I speak with her in privacy."

"Yes Mother, you are quite right," Mary said. "I see you have arrived upon a strategy to deal with the situation. Since Emmie has not brought up the topic of marriage with us, we will have to be the ones to open the conversation. What will you say?"

"I plan to start by letting her know that we understand her predicament. After all, her parents did not tell her that they had expectations of her becoming engaged so she has had no time to prepare herself. However, we cannot turn the clock back and we must take the situation as it stands today."

"I think that is very wise, Mother," Mary replied, "As it will do Emmie good to know we understand how she must feel."

"Emmie is old enough and mature enough to think things through. She does not need a lecture on obedience to her parents. I will simply ask her to consider her own well being for the future. I want to reassure her that Willie and Bel are quite fine for the time being. However, they will not live forever and we never know what is the allotted time that the Lord has given us. They cannot help but look ahead for the future security of their children."

"This is true indeed." Mary agreed. "Young people are so tied up in the joys of today and think little for the wants of tomorrow."

"I will suggest to Emmie that the best thing she could do for her parents is to think about herself and her future for a change. They would want her to thoroughly enjoy her visit and not to be moping about conditions at home. It is a time to be gay and jolly with the young people."

"Well, do you think that will be enough? Mary queried. "Do you plan to discuss the topic of marriage directly?"

"Oh yes," Sophia added, "I will lay the cards on the table. I will point out that since her mother is not here I would hope that she could confide in us who love her dearly regarding anything that troubles her about the prospect of married life. Perhaps she is frightened about childbirth or intimate relations or who knows what could be on her mind?"

"Dear me, Mother!" Mary gasped. "Perhaps that is being just a little too forward!"

"Why should it be? The girl has lived around dairy cattle and livestock in Canada. She is not so citified as to be ignorant of the score."

"But.... but Mother," Mary stammered, "It's one thing to know about animals... and quite another to discuss what goes on in the privacy of the bedroom."

"It's not my intention to probe if she is not disposed to talking. But perhaps Emmie has never had the opportunity and might be relieved to have a 'woman to woman' talk. Given how red she gets when the boys tease her, it wouldn't surprise me if Emmie would benefit from a chance to bring her cares out into the open with women who are experienced. Bottling things up inside is clearly not doing her any good."

"You are indeed wise Mother. I had not thought of it that way. I will call over to Sunville and ask Phoebe to see that Emmie comes for tea alone tomorrow. No doubt she will have an inkling what we are up to."

Emmie Has a Chance to Air Her Feelings

As Mary Boyd opened the cast iron oven door, the kitchen at Bracken Brae filled with the heavenly smell of fresh baked scones. Mary was keen that today's Tea should be especially nice. She had set the best china out on the tea trolley and filled little dishes with homemade strawberry jam and Cleeve's rich clotted cream. A plate of fancy cucumber and watercress sandwiches topped off today's fare. As Mary fussed over the arrangement of her culinary creations, she heard the faint tinkle of the bell from the front of the house.

"Oh, that will be Emmie now." But today Mary's face was pinched, suggesting an air of apprehension instead of her usual jolly demeanour. Mary trundled the tea trolley into the parlour in time to hear Emmie bid Sophia a cheerful good afternoon.

"Mmmm....fresh baked scones. I see that I've arrived just in time. It's only me today, Aunt. Phoebe is still in town with the girls at the dressmaker's. Though I am well pleased to be here under your cozy roof as it is surely going to rain. There are dark clouds moving in and I've heard thunder in the distance."

"Well, do sit down and have a nice cup of tea," Sophia cooed in her soft Irish brogue. "We'll have all these scones to ourselves and the rain will not stop us from having a jolly tea party."

"Here you are Mother," Mary chirped as she handed a steaming cup of tea to Sophia. "Have a cucumber sandwich."

"Oh, cucumber sandwiches too! My favourite! You will make me fat," Emmie laughed.

"Help yourself, Cousin. Eat up," Mary urged. "There's no fear of ruining your lovely figure. You could even do well with a pound or two more."

Sofia donned her spectacles as she picked up a letter from the table beside her. "We've had a letter this morning from your mother, Emmie. You'll be pleased to know that all is well in Canada and there is no need for any worry. She says to tell you that Harry and Ben have been a great help and that the gardens have produced a bumper crop this year."

"Oh," Emmie interrupted, "She will need me to help put up the stores for the winter, then."

"Well she says not, Emmie," Sophia countered. "Here...she says that Blanche Aylmer and the MacKenzie girls have offered to help. Willie and the boys will come home at the weekend to harvest and do the heavy lifting. She says to tell you that all is taken care of and that you must continue to enjoy your stay in Ireland."

"But Aunt,", Emmie argued as her face darkened, "I just MUST get home!"

Sophia offered a firm rebuttal, "Your mother clearly says there is no rush, dear child. Now tell us what is REALLY bothering you. I can see that you are upset and I do hope that you could unburden yourself to Mary and me."

Mary added, "While it's true that we could never replace your dear mother, perhaps this is a time when you have need of a motherly presence. We may be a poor substitute but I fear we are all you have got right now."

Sophia adopted a conciliatory manner. "Yes, Emmie. Mary is right. I fear we are no match for dear Bel, but we are concerned for you and truly wish to offer you an opportunity to air your feelings. It cannot but do harm if you bottle up whatever is bothering you. I wonder if there is anything you wish to discuss about....well Phoebe told us that Frank proposed marriage and that you turned him down."

Feeling compassion for Emmie's obvious distress, Mary pleaded, "Dear cousin, if ever a young woman needed a mother's wise counsel, it is now. A proposal of marriage is no light occasion. As your mother's dearest friend, it is my duty to hear you out."

Emmie stammered as she searched for words. "Well...I'm....well I don't want anyone to think I am ungrateful. You and Tom and Phoebe have been most kind. ALL of the Cleeves have welcomed me with open arms. But the truth is, I do feel I was sent to Ireland under false pretenses."

"False pretenses?", Sophia queried. "What false pretenses do you mean?"

Emmie spoke in a halting voice. "Well Frank told me that Father is penniless and that I must be some sort of ninny if I didn't realize that I'd been sent to Ireland to find a husband. I swear, Aunt....Father said not one word about marriage. Nor Mother either. I feel so humiliated! If I'd known that I was expected to marry, I would never have come here."

"Poor dear child!", Sophia commiserated. "Frank should never have said that. But I suppose that his ego was bruised and he just lashed out. And you are perfectly in the right, dear. It was very wrong of your parents not to make their expectations clear."

Emmie fought back tears as she complained, "Now I am stuck here. Evidently, Father has turned me out and I am dependant on the good will of the Cleeve family."

"I must ask you," Sophia broke in. "Was your refusal of Frank's proposal a response to your parents' deception? Are you quite sure that you do not wish to marry Frank?"

"I do not wish to marry ANYONE!" Emmie retorted. "Why can I not be left in peace?"

Somewhat startled, Sophia queried, "Tell me dear child, is there anything about marriage that frightens you? You are so capable of running a household and so good with children...."

Emmie interrupted with irritation, "I just want to be in MY home, with MY family, helping to run MY household!! Mother is so burdened on her own looking after a house full of men."

Mary interjected, "Well, I certainly know THAT situation. Remember that I was also the only girl in a house full of boys! I was constantly being teased by my brothers. The worst was when I began to develop a womanly figure. Lordie, there was no end to their chaff!"

"Father doesn't allow the boys to get away with any nonsense," Emmie replied. "Besides, I have learned to hold my own and can give any one of them a good solid blow."

Sophia decided she would have to venture into delicate territory. "Tell me, dear child, is it possible that you are frightened of childbirth?"

"To be honest, Aunt, I hadn't really thought about that. I just have never pictured myself having children of my own."

"Well then....," Sophia persisted, "Forgive me for asking....but has your mother never discussed with you the womanly duties involved with marital relations?"

Emmie spluttered and coughed as she choked on her tea. "Good God! Must I answer that?" Emmie turned crimson with embarrassment as Mary rushed to her side to mop up spilt tea.

"Please don't Mary," Emmie responded in a broken voice. " I can manage on my own. I just need to get some air."

Emmie made a dash for the front door as she continued to cough. In an instant she found herself out in the afternoon's drizzle. Without her realizing it, Emmie's feet suddenly took over and began to carry her rapidly away from the scene of her embarrassment. Before long, she was running along the North Circular Road towards Sunville House. Startled by a loud thunderclap and ensuing cloudburst, Emmie took refuge under a large Yew tree.

"God help me!", Emmie pleaded out loud... "What am I to do? Even my closest female companions betray me. Why will they not leave me be? I do not wish to marry ANYBODY. Must I submit to the will of some man just because THEY have all done so? I would sooner die than be forced into marriage!"

Emmie broke down sobbing, unaware that she had begun to shiver in her soaking wet clothes. Strands of wet hair hung limply over her face as she peered into the distance at a figure approaching with an umbrella. Realizing that it was Phoebe Cleeve, Emmie forced herself to stop crying and attempted to regain some composure.

"Oh Emmie," Phoebe gasped, "Whatever has come over you? Look at you – you are soaked to the bone! Mary telephoned to say that you had run off into the rain without any protection. Here, put this shawl around your shoulders and come close under my umbrella. We must get you home into a warm bath."

Feeling wretched and embarrassed, Emmie succumbed to the comfort of rescue and the warmth of Phoebe's body next to her. She could not bring herself to explain how she had arrived in her current predicament as her throat closed over in shame. Phoebe, in turn, was wise enough to gently guide Emmie home without demanding any explanation. She would talk to Mary and Mother Cleeve another day to sort out what to do next. For the time being, Phoebe's intuition told her to give Emmie a few days to recover.

Emmie Continues a Letter to Her Mother – Minus a Few Details

August 6th

Just got your Post Card. I was getting quite anxious as it is twelve days since I heard from home. I do miss you all and am so homesick. I pray that we will be together again soon!

I have been in Town to get fitted. My blouse will be finished tomorrow and in my next letter will send a piece of the stuff. On my way out of town, I stopped in to Bracken Brae to see Mary and Aunt Sofia and we had a long chat. On the way back to Sunville, I was caught in a downpour and got soaked to the bone. Dear Cousin Phoebe came to my rescue with an umbrella and shawl and I am none the worse for wear.

Saturday 7th

It is one o'clock. I have just come in from Town. I drove in with Cousin Tom at nine, had my blouse fitted, then went to the dentist. He hurt me much and I am not nearly finished.

I have not seen Miss King yet, as when she came, I was in Town. Frank went in for her. She told him the Rev. Andrew Balfour was staying with them and saw her off, and that he said he knew me very well. I had no idea Mr. Balfour was on this side of the water. After all, the world is small!

Only one of the Miss Kings, the one who wrote to me, is here at Sunville. The other wrote last night to say she could not leave her mother. Miss King is a very English girl, full of fun. She is twenty-three and dresses beautifully. Frank is quite her devoted admirer. We tease him a lot about that.

Yesterday evening we had great fun at home. We girls led Frank a fine dance. Then we all had a pillow fight and a fight with the stockings Phoebe was mending. The others are all too strong for me, but I have my revenge by tickling. Lil is dreadfully ticklish and will scream if you touch her.

Cousin Phoebe asked me to help her to make out the Bill of Farm for Wednesday market day. It is a very swell event. The fruit will come from London. I will wear my velvet dress. Phoebe said I am such a big help to her and that she wishes I could be here always.

My blouse will be finished tonight. I am sending you a piece of the stuff. It seems to fit nicely. I know you will be glad to hear my hip is well. I walked in from Town yesterday and today and do not feel tired - about two miles. I suppose it would ache if I did too much, but I will be careful.

Cousin Dawse arrived this morning and the girls rode around to see him. He is much thinner than he used to be; he is quite an Englishman, and handsome. I am so sorry that Ruth is quite badly hurt. Her face and body are bruised and foot sprained. The Doctor has her in bed so she could not come.

Uncle Ben is quite well again. Jenny Cleeve also came home last night from Dublin. Olive brought me a lovely pair of thick soft leather gloves yesterday for a birthday present. She said, had I told her when my birthday was, I would have had them earlier.

I am so brown now as I am out all the time about the place without a hat. How I envy these two girls their lovely clear complexions without a spot, but I have no pimples now and look very strong. I am always being told how fat I am. I must close now and dress for lunch - will wear a low dress later tonight.

Goodbye darling Mother. Love and kisses to the boys. Your loving child,

      Emily

     ~~~~~

NINE

Disaster Strikes

Young Ben Misses His Sister

I miss dear Emmie. When is she going to find her 'old man' and then come home to us? I wish she would get on with it. She has been gone ever so long! And she was not home for her birthday so there was no cake to share. Hasn't been any cake lately. Ma says there is no money for cake because Pa's work does not pay well and we are poor now. I don't like being poor.

I wish we could have our store back. There was always money for sweets and cakes when Pa had the store. I guess I will have to write to Em and tell her there was no money to pay the June school fees. I don't like writing letters. The only good thing about being poor is that Harry and I don't have to go to school. We get to play when we don't have to do chores.

Emmie wrote and said we must help Ma all we can while Pa is away. I wish Pa would come home too, and Eddie and Dick. I want things to be like they were before. Now there's so much work for Harry and me to do. I shall tell Emmie to hurry up and get home to us and bake a lovely cake like she always used to do. Maybe if I tell her we are just about starving to death she will send us a cake from Ireland. Ma says the people Emmie is staying with are very rich and maybe she will marry one of them.

Emmie's Last Letter – "If only I could have been kissed by you all"

Sunville

August 9th 1897

My Dear Harry and Ben,

I think it is quite time to write to you two boys. It was very sweet of you to write to me for my birthday. The letters came in while I was at breakfast, so I did indeed feel the love and all the fond wishes. If only I could have been kissed by you all, how happy I should have been.

(In pencil on the back: "Written the morning she was taken ill")

Phoebe Cleeve Expresses Distress Over Emmie's Serious Condition

Lord God! What are we to do? Surely it is not the Lord's will that this lovely girl should be taken in the prime of her life and in our home. Emmie's parents have entrusted her to our care and all we can do is stand by helplessly watching the life ebb from her young frame. This surely is the greatest catastrophe to ever befall the Cleeve household.

How will I ever find the words to deliver such a sorrowful

message to Dear Bel and Willie? God cannot be so cruel as to take their only daughter from them. Have they not been sufficiently afflicted? Bel's father has been in his grave barely two years now, and then her dear mother followed not six months later. Then that dreadful fire took the family store and Willie's source of livelihood with it. Willie, Eddie, and Dick are scattered hither and yon unable to find decent work, and now Emmie is gravely ill so very far from home.

Still, Dr Fogarty works on indefatigably saying, "Where there is life there is hope". Perhaps it is wicked of me to think the worst. Perhaps, by some miracle, the dear girl will rally and pull through. Surely God will not take Emmie too, for it is just too much to bear. Fogarty has told her that her condition is very serious. She took it so calmly and said if anything happens, bury me by cousin Janie under the big beech tree.

Tom has already gone ahead and made the arrangements with Lord Aylmer to have the grave beside his daughter Jane in the Cathedral cemetery. I begged him not to be too hasty but he insisted that he must insure that the dear child's last wish be granted else there will surely be a fire awaiting him in hell when his time comes. Tom insists there is a look in the doctor's eyes that gives away his true sentiment and there is no hope for dear Emmie.

Still I must write Bel by this morning's mail and warn her. It is Emmie's day to write home and Bel will wonder why she has not had a letter from her. Perhaps the tide will turn after all. I must not be too harsh in my description of the situation. I must not give in. I must have faith and pray to God that Emmie will be spared.

Phoebe Cleeve Writes to Emmie's Mother

Sunville House

14th August 1897.

My Dear Bel,

As your darling child is unable to write by the usual Saturday mail, I cannot allow it to pass without giving you some idea of what has occurred since the memorable Monday when she took so suddenly ill. She ate a good breakfast, then went in to the kitchen, made buns, and a couple of shapes as we were contemplating a gypsy tea to Castle Connell. I then went in to the kitchen when Emmie left. I thought she looked flushed, but as it was a holiday, thought it was the heat of the kitchen. She did not complain then.

She went upstairs to start a letter to you. After some time I asked Lil if she would ask Em to cut some cucumber sandwiches. Then Lil came and told me she was complaining of a pain in her side. At the time I did not think much of it till Lil came running for mustard to make a plaister.

It was only the work of an instant to get Tom and send for the doctor, so remedies were used at once and I hardly tell you everything that human care and knowledge can, has been done for the dear child. Each day we dreaded, being afraid it might be her last, but yesterday and today we have a glimmer of hope but cannot yet be sure until the stomach is less distended than it is at present. She is now living on whiskey and nutrient enemas, as other things are inclined to cause sickness.

Weakness is her great trouble, as whatever pain she may have is not acute. I thought she might wish to send on what she had written, but she said no, it would not be worth sending. She would keep it till she was able to add more. When the doctor told her of her serious condition, she took it so calmly, and spoke of you once or twice to Mary who is indefatigable in her attention to her.

I hope and pray that her state may continue to improve and that each day may bring you better news than the last. I do pity you so much being separated from her. Your feelings must be awful. All join me in love and sympathy to you and yours.

Believe me dear Bel

To be your fond cousin,

Phoebe

P.S. Em sends her love to you all and hopes soon to be able to write. I will write again on Wednesday.

Mary Cleeve Boyd Prepares to Write a Sad Letter

How will I ever find the words to tell my dearest friend what has happened here? I can barely comprehend it myself, let alone convey such desolate news to the darling child's mother. I must ask God to give me the strength and to guide my hand in writing this saddest of letters. I must tell her all that was done for dear Emmie so Bel can rest assured that no effort was spared in trying to save her precious child.

Bel is a good Christian woman and will bear this affliction as she has all others. God will give her the strength to live on. She must for the sake of Willie and the boys. Uncle Ben is right when he says that Emmie was an angel and "God had need of her."

She was such a sweet child and if ever there was need of an angel in heaven, Emmie would fit the bill.

I dare say I am exhausted in the wake of this severe trial. Phoebe and Tom are terribly cut up. They will need a good rest by the seaside. Such a dreadful thing to have the poor dear die in their house. But I suppose they must take some solace from the fact that Emmie was surrounded by loving relatives in her last days. It's the very best we could do when she was separated by an ocean from those dearest to her heart. How my heart aches when I recall her crying out "Mother", "Father" in the midst of her suffering. The one thing she longed for most, we could not give her.

Willie and Bel must be asking themselves if they did the right thing by sending Emmie overseas. If only they had sent her to the doctor to look into that pain in her hip before she came over. Dr. Fogarty said it was too late to do the surgery by the time he saw poor Emmie. The appendix had already ruptured and death would have been a certainty if he had operated then. As it was, there wasn't much chance of survival once the poor child's body became septic. We had to bury her so quickly to remove any contagion from Tom and Phoebe's house. After all, there was the safety of their own children to consider. 'Tis a pity that we could not send Emmie home to be buried with her family but the doctors said it would be too dangerous and the corpse could not withstand the journey under the circumstances. It makes me shudder to think of it.

Still, we can take solace that Emmie's last wish was granted. She lies in eternal rest beside her young cousin Jane Aylmer. It was terribly good of Lord Aylmer to give Tom the grave for Emmie. Perhaps it will give him some peace as well to know that his dear daughter has a companion. He and Emily's grandmother, Louisa Journeaux, were first cousins. It is just as well that Louisa, God rest her soul, did not live to see this day. She was so petted on Emily.

How upset Louisa would have been to know that Emily did not live to marry and have a daughter. She used to talk about Emmie carrying on the line of women that are descended from her Portuguese ancestor who nearly became a martyr in the Inquisition. Frankly, I have to wonder if there is any truth to that story. But it's true that Louisa's mother was born in Portuguese India; at least we know that much of a certainty.

Enough of all this rambling. I dare say it's an excuse to put off the inevitable. When all is said and done, I am still left with the duty to write to my dear cousin and make some attempt, no matter how feeble, to comfort her. Ah but Life can be so cruel!

Mary Cleeve Boyd's Letter to Bel Woodburn

Bracken Brae

August 17th 1897

My Dearest Bel,

How to write and express my grief and sympathy for you and Willie is beyond me. I do trust God will give you strength to live after such a sorrow as I know yours must be. We all know she was the dear one and the pet of you all at home. There has not been one to hear of it but to express the greatest sympathy for her poor mother. She had endeared herself to all that had met her. Poor mother is terrible cut up for love of dear Emmie and grief for you.

The last day she was here was the Friday afternoon before she was taken ill and mother, Miss Haddlesy, and I were having a cup of afternoon tea. Emmie comes up to the window laughing and taps at it and says they were just in time. Phoebe and Frank were with her. Phoebe was very fond of Emmie and as kind and good to her as she could be.

Sunday I met dear Emmie again at Fernbank at afternoon tea. The men all went into the house and she and I sat outside to have a chat. I had been saying to her not to look so sad and then when we were alone she said to me, "Do you know Mary, I feel as if something very bad was hanging over me." I told her not to be silly, nothing was going to happen, she just was out of sorts, for sometimes she used to get you on her mind and would feel lonely, and I always tried to laugh her out of her low spirits.

After that I did not see her until Monday morning about half past twelve. Lil came after me that her mother was frightened about Emmie. She had been taken with great pain. They had telephoned for the doctor and he was on his way out. He and I got there almost at the same time.

Emmie had been helping Phoebe get ready to go to a gypsy tea and had no pain so far as anyone knows up to half past eleven. I knew by the Dr.'s face it was a very bad case. He was there five times that day and three times every other day. They also had a second doctor in to consult. The two that were with Emmie are considered the two cleverest in Limerick. We all think Fogerty as clever as can be got- and they say Kennedy is just as good.

They had a trained nurse at once and Phoebe and I both took charge of her while the nurse was sleeping. I stayed with Emmie from before ten in the mornings until seven in the evenings each day she was ill. I never left the room during that time. I would try and send Phoebe about the house, for she would be up and down all the nights to see Emmie was all right (for the nurse took charge at night). Emmie was never left for one second alone from the time she got ill.

Friday we got hope she seemed to be a shade better and the doctor seemed more cheerful, but in the afternoon, I felt it was a false hope, for I saw signs I did not like, but I did not tell him or Phoebe as they were so anxious and I knew everything was being done that could be. After the first couple of days she could take nothing by her mouth, so every four hours she got an injection of the yolk of an egg, half a wine glass of the juice of beef, half a wine glass of whey. She got a teaspoon of whiskey by her mouth every half hour. It was mixed with water - only a teaspoon, water and all.

Then Saturday evening she took a decided change for the worse and Sunday morning we gave up all hope. All the same, the Dr. worked on and did his best. He said as long as there was life we must work. He spent a lot of time each time he was out on Sunday. We knew the end was near so I sat up with the nurse Sunday night and did not leave her again.

She died at five minutes past ten Monday morning. She never spoke after about half past eleven Sunday morning. I think she knew me when I went in first. She put her arms round my neck and for me to kiss her. When your letter arrived early in the week she would not try to read it at first, for she said to me. I don't want to break down, so as to try and get well. Then after a time she said I'll try and read it but her eyes must have been dim, for she could not see, so she told me to put it in the envelope and leave it under her pillow until she was better.

So both your letters and Eddie's were not read. I read your card to her and mother had a letter from Bel Aylmer and I took it over and read it to her. (Bel had said in it that you were well and in good spirits). On Saturday night she was calling to you a lot and she called her father. Nurse said Sunday, she called "Mother, Mother" several times.

About the last thing she said was, I beg your pardon Doctor. She had a habit of throwing her hands over her head, and she hit his spectacles. The Dr. took a great interest in her and at the early stage of her illness he told me he'd do his utmost to save her, for I told him what a very precious child she was to you all. The Dr. told her she was very ill indeed, but I fancy she would not allow herself to think of dying in case she'd break down.

I asked her, not as if I thought seriously of her sickness, would she like to send any message and she said no, only tell mother to take care of herself. And another time she said if anything should happen to me, bury me by Janie Aylmer and she wanted them to be careful about breaking the news to you. The dear child suffered a good deal and wandered a good deal off and on from Wednesday out.

One thing, dear Bel you can make your mind happy about, every mortal thing that could be done for her was done by Tom and Phoebe, and Phoebe was as affectionate and thoughtful as if it were Eileen or Lil. Emmie liked the nurse very much and was quite happy with her. She was a very nice kind girl and never spared herself any trouble. We were all very pleased with her.

Phoebe and I helped the nurse to wash her and lay her out. Tom, Ted, and Fred saw to putting her in the coffin and all the

Cleeve boys helped carry her to the hearse and grave, so only loving hands had to do with your dear child.

The coffin dear Emmie was put in was a lovely one. I never saw as nice a one before and there were a good many wreaths and crosses. Eileen made a wreath and two crosses. Tom and Phoebe had a lovely wreath made, so had Fred and Jennie, Mother, Jack and I sent a cross I made myself. The coffin was covered with nice flowers. They had the funeral private, just a few intimate friends besides our own boys. Several sent their carriages. I hope the photos of the coffin will be good. Tom and Phoebe thought you would like to have one.

Why I have not mentioned Joe and Kathleen up to this, they were away on their holiday. Joe tried to be home for the funeral but the boat from England missed the train and he was late. Kathleen was too upset to come.

I have written you all these details, hoping it would be a shadow of comfort to you my dear Bel. We will all be most anxious to hear how you are and Willie. Of course I know the boys will feel it bitterly but it can't equal the parent's grief. Any questions you like to ask, I will answer to the best of my ability.

Now my dear Bel, I must stop. Trusting God will support you in this severe grief (I mean poor Willie too). I do feel for you both from the depth of my heart. Jack joins me in my sympathy for you both. He was very fond of dear Emmie and very grieved about her. She liked Jack too. Mother will write when she feels equal to it. She is very upset. Goodbye and may God bless you all.

Ever your loving and sympathizing cousin,
Mary Boyd

Phoebe Cleeve Writes to Bel Woodburn

Now that we are returned from the seaside and a much-needed respite, I must write to Bel and say a few things I had not previously mentioned. Oh, why did they not have her seen by a doctor before coming out? If only we could have known what was wrong we might have saved the poor girl. If she had had the operation before the appendix ruptured she might have survived. But then again, how could we have taken on the responsibility of making that decision? Even if we had cabled, Willie might not have given permission for the surgery to proceed. And what if she'd had the operation and died anyway? We might have been blamed for that.

I wish I knew what was in Bel and Willie's minds and how they are weathering this great trial. I would have thought I'd have heard from Bel by now. But maybe they are all too grief-stricken to put pen to paper. Lord, I pray that they do not hold it against us. Surely they must believe that everything that was humanly possible was done for dear Emmie. Lil and Eileen are devastated and Mother Cleeve is inconsolable. I suppose everyone grieves in their own way, for Frank has been very quiet.

Mother had such high hopes of a match between Emmie and Frank but I do not think that Em ever really warmed up to him, nor to any young man, for that matter. It was strange, I don't know what to make of her seeming shyness with the young men when she was so outgoing with the older folk.

And my dear husband, Tom, was so terribly fond of Emmie. I dare say he thought of her as if she were his own child. No expense was spared for her medical care and the coffin Tom chose was one of the finest I've seen. Too bad that the nature of her illness required us to bury her so quickly with no time for a proper funeral. But I take solace in the fact that only loving hands touched her once she was gone, even if it was hard on us all. Ah, it will be a long time before the pall of gloom is lifted from this household.

I must put pen to paper:

Sunville House, Limerick

8th September 1897.

Dear Bel,

On Tuesday I visited your darling's resting place; it looked very peaceful. On the first Sunday Emmie went to the Cathedral, I took her to see Jane Aylmer's grave. Who would have thought that she would so soon be laid there? Oh, the uncertainty of life!

I suppose Mary told you how depressed she felt on the Sunday. I can't but think she was not feeling well. Certainly she did not complain, only of feeling chilly. Had Dr. Fogarty been at house, I should have taken her in after we came first from Dublin. She complained so often of a pain in her side and of a great feeling of weakness, but it passed off and latterly she seemed to be and looked much better.

How we looked forward to the return of the young people. She said when she saw them kissing me, it made her long for a Mother's kiss. She told me she wrote you the same thing. We had many a long chat about her home and she showed me such devotion to all under the much loved roof. I don't think she liked the idea of leaving the old house where you had all been so happy for such a long time, to go to Montreal. Then the darling child was so exercised in her mind when Uncle Ben wished her to spend the winter with them; she thought it awfully good of them, "But I can't leave Mother," she said, "The winter would be so lonely for her without Father."

The day the Dr. told her she was in a very critical condition, she seemed to understand that she was to do everything to husband her strength. She did not seem to care to speak of anything about death for fear of breaking down. She showed such strength of will to live. She was pleased when the Dr. decided on not having an operation. Then after that, she seemed to get less conscious. One night the nurse said she was repeating hymns and said "I am coming, 'tis very hard to go".

If ever there was a girl fit for the bright world, she was. Did Mary tell you of something she said to Ted on the Sunday before she took ill? I know he made use of some strong language and Em read him a lecture. Ted replied, "Ah! Emmie you are too good to live". "No Ted, no one is too good to live", said she.

I remember so well walking round the garden after supper on that Sunday with our arms round one another and she saying to me, "Now the girls have returned, I do not seem to get you to myself at all". We had a few turns before Tom took me off to Bracken Brae. I saw her next that night when we came home, in bed with Lillie. They were awake talking.

I hoped to have had a letter saying how you all were before this, but suppose I shall soon hear. All join me in love, Believe me dear Bel,

Your fond cousin,

                Phoebe

Letter of Condolence from Uncle Ben Journeaux

15 Palmerston Road, Rathmines

August 18th, 1897

Dear Isabella,

I have no need to tell you how we feel for you, Willie, and your boys. I find it hard even to express our sympathy. You know how we loved Dear Em and how she loved us. You can well understand how, and with what pleasure we were looking forward to having her with us. But we know Our Heavenly Father does not willingly afflict and that He has a wise purpose in all He does. The older we grow, the more proof we have of His tender love.

You know of old what a favourite Em was with us all. I have entered my 77th year and cannot expect to be long after her. One great comfort you can look forward to is having your four sons, and our trust is that they may be long spared to you.

Please write me two lines when you can. You know you have our true sympathy and also that of all your old and true friends around you. We hope before making any change you will let us know as Old Friends are the truest, and moving is very costly. Your Aunt sends you her fond love and sympathy. Trusting Our Heavenly Father may support and comfort you, Willie, and the boys,

I remain your loving Old Uncle,

    Ben Journeaux

Note to Thomas Cleeve from Willie Woodburn

5th October 1898

The following was sent to Mr. T.H. Cleeve, Sunville House, Limerick, Ireland,

To be inscribed on our darling's tombstone:

Emily
daughter of
Wm. J. and Isabella Woodburn
born in
Melbourne Canada
27th July 1873
died in Limerick
16th August 1897
"Gone Home! now resting calmly
amid the loved ones there.
Gone Home! to be with Jesus
Mid all that's bright and fair."

Flash Forward to November 2006

Liz Woodburn Visits Emmie's Grave in Limerick

Over a century has passed. With the previous letters in hand, I find myself in Limerick at Emmie's graveside. It feels quite strange to be visiting a grave that appears to be someone else's but is also my own - takes some doing to wrap one's mind around being BOTH dead and alive! Yet I believe it to be so. Perhaps it is just as well we don't have full consciousness of past lives. It is difficult enough to manage being one person, never mind being someone else too!

And so many emotions are swirling around in my consciousness. I feel everyone's grief over a shocking death, including Emmie's distress for those she left behind. Yet I am also very aware of her anger when recalling my recent experience on the pathway outside the Kilmainham Gaol. Emmie meant it when she said that she would rather die than be forced into an unwanted marriage. Today I feel regret for what might have been. Yet there is no going back – only moving forward. I have returned to a sticking point and desire to set things right. I must give Emmie her voice!

This is now possible because so much has happened in a hundred years! The gravestones nearby are evidence that the Cleeve family members that Emmie knew have all lived out their lives and died. I am surprised to find that Willie Woodburn's request for the tombstone inscription was not granted. Perhaps Thomas Cleeve and Lord Aylmer agreed there wasn't room for everything that Willie Woodburn wanted to include. Instead, Emmie is briefly mentioned at the bottom of the stone, almost like an afterthought:

"EMILY, Daughter of Wm. J. Woodburn. Died 16th Aug 1897, Aged 24 years."

Today I am pleased to see that Willie did not get his way. He was determined to have it that Emmie should be with 'some man' in a distant home caring for her family! I cannot say for certain who the final arbiter was in settling on the tombstone inscription, but it strikes me that this is closer to what Emmie would have wanted with the exception that her mother's name is not mentioned. In a way, I feel quite smug now to see that Emmie has been memorialized as 'her father's daughter' without any flowery verses. Plain and simple – for I am just as stubborn as he is!

Mind you, it is fair enough to say that stubbornness can also be seen as tenacity. Through determination and perseverance Willie succeeded in restoring his standard of living soon after Emmie's death. He abandoned any thought of rebuilding the store in Melbourne and relocated with the family to Montreal.

By 1912 all of the Woodburn boys had married. Willie and Bel both died in 1922 within six months of each other. Eddie died suddenly of a heart attack in 1926. Dick moved to London, England with his bride and had three children. He died in 1953, having lived to see his grandchildren.

Harry married in 1907. Sadly, his wife died of tuberculosis three years later. Harry had become infected and died in a TB sanatorium in 1913. Ben married his best friend's cousin, Bessie Reynolds, in 1911. They had three children in all but only one, my father, survived childhood. Dad married in 1943 in the middle of the second World War.

Just as the context of the Victorian era was vital to Emmie's life story, the rapid and far-reaching social changes that occurred during the twentieth century set the tone for a new lifetime. I will digress to trace historic events that paved the way to my birth in 1948.

~~~~~

TEN

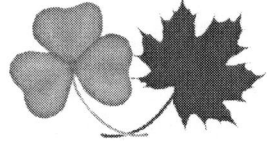

Back To The Future

Afterward

If Emmie had lived out a normal lifespan, she would have witnessed sweeping changes, especially where women's rights and opportunities were concerned. In 1897, the year of Emmie's death, a monumental event toward the advancement of women occurred in London, England. Seventeen campaign groups joined forces to form The National Union of Women's Suffrage Societies. A few courageous women had become activists in speaking up publicly for the right to vote for women. Soon others followed, creating a groundswell that reverberated throughout the Western world. Women were speaking up!

By 1920 President Woodrow Wilson introduced the 19th Amendment into the American Constitution, prohibiting gender-based restrictions on voting. In 1928, British women were granted the right to vote on the same terms as men. Other Western countries followed suit and by 1948, voting rights for women were introduced into International Law by the United Nations via the

Universal Declaration of Human Rights.

In ever increasing numbers, women fought for the right to higher education. It followed that women were entering professions where they had previously been barred like medicine and law. We began to see women entering into politics and becoming a voice in government. However, for the average woman, child-bearing and housework were still her main lot in life.

It took two world wars to prove that women were capable of doing just about any job that a man could do. As men went off to war in the 1940's, women were being recruited by the hundreds of thousands to support the war effort at home. In Canada, 'Ronnie the Bren Gun Girl' represented the new look in glamour for women. The now infamous 'Rosie the Riveter' was the poster girl for American bravado and patriotism.

When peace was declared in September of 1945, it was estimated that over seventy million people, both military and civilian, had perished. As surviving soldiers returned home, men once again became the predominant work force. Nature took its course and a population explosion known as the 'post war baby boom' returned women to the primary tasks of childcare and domestic drudgery.

Since my father had been unfit for military service due to his heart condition, he contributed to the war effort through his job in the food industry. As was expected in those days, my mother had given up her job as a school secretary in 1943 when she married Dad. The role of wife and mother turned out to be a disaster for Mom as she didn't like children or housework. She missed the independence she had enjoyed while single and employed. Mom was deeply unhappy and fought constantly with Dad about her desire to go out to work.

Old ideas die hard, and both Dad and my Grampa Ben insisted that it would bring shame on the family if Mom took even a part time job. People would think that Dad was incapable of supporting his family. Besides, the war had been an unusual circumstance and 'working women' were just unnatural. The beliefs that 'a woman's place is in the home' and that 'men are the money managers' continued to rule our household.

Prior to marriage, my mother had enjoyed her career and paycheque. Quite understandably she resented not having access to money after her marriage. I often wondered why the issue of finances had not been discussed when Mom and Dad were courting, but it seems to have been pretty common in those days to jump into marriage without clarity about the expectations of one's prospective mate.

Mom had also been raised with servants and had very little experience with housework, laundry and menial chores. She had no experience at all with child-rearing or babysitting so the realities of dirty diapers, screaming infants, and defiant toddlers came as a complete shock. The net result was a very angry and frustrated woman who felt trapped and resentful towards her children. Not surprisingly, Mom took her anger out on my brother and me and we were subjected to beatings, daily verbal abuse and death threats.

The seeds of low self-esteem were sown early in my life with a litany of name-calling: retardate, congenital idiot, cretin, trollop, flousie, nuisance, pest etc. etc. Mom only did this during the daytime when Dad was out at work. She saw it as her duty to maintain a pleasant atmosphere in the home once Dad returned from work. This was supposedly meant to prevent undue strain on Dad's heart. However, the result was an extremely skewed view of parental authority where Dad was the knight in shining armour and Mom was the cruel wicked witch.

In spite of her sense of oppression, Mom had a paradoxical attitude towards men. She always referred to her father, the church minister, or family doctor as though they were wise and all knowing. Her usual explanation for why we children should do something was because some man said so. No doubt, this had been her childhood training and was an ingrained response that she did not question.

I cannot say how other children in our community were treated by their parents. One never knows what really goes on behind closed doors. I suspect that most of my contemporaries were dealing with the aftermath of stresses brought on by their parents' experiences during the war. Many of the men had seen battle, women had experienced privation, and every family had lost loved ones. In those days there was no such thing as counselling for post-traumatic stress.

My father's best friend had been killed during the war as well as a cousin and some childhood friends. Yet, these painful losses were never spoken of, especially in the presence of children. It was as though people wanted to shut the door on the past. People just got on with their lives and hoped to build a happy future.

Post War Baby Boom

Whenever the women in my childhood neighbourhood got together, conversation always led to the latest theories on child rearing. It was then inevitable that horror stories about the birth of their incorrigible children would follow. Ever keen to dramatize the events of her life, my mother would trot out the story of my birth:

"It seems I had committed the ultimate faux pas of being ready to deliver before the doctor had arrived at the hospital. The delivery rooms were all occupied and the anaesthetist was run off his feet. I tried to tell them I could deliver the child naturally right in the bed but no one would listen. A matronly voice ordered me NOT to push as she barked out to the nurses, 'Cross her legs!' The last thing I remember was a strong muscular arm coming down across my chest as a chloroformed rag was thrust over my nose. When I came to, it was all over. The nurse showed me the baby and then whisked her off to the nursery.

Frank was in the waiting room with the other fathers. He was thrilled to have a girl this time. Mind you, if the first baby four years ago hadn't been a boy, they would have just had to put it back! Of course, Frank's parents were even more excited this time to have a girl in the family.

They'd had an awful time where children were concerned. Their first child was stillborn at home. Another one was run over by a car when he was four years old....died in his mother's arms on the way to the hospital. And then Frank nearly died when he contracted rheumatic fever as a teen-ager. His heart was left badly damaged and it's a miracle he survived to have children at all!"

Another of Mom's stories had to do with my name. I was told that Grampa Ben was the youngest of four boys. He'd had one sister, Emmie, who had been sent to Ireland to find a husband. The family was devastated when she died suddenly of a ruptured appendix without accomplishing that goal. I was supposed to have been named after Grampa's sister but his excitement quickly turned to horror when he realized we had the same birthday. He was superstitious and believed it was an ill omen that I'd been born on Emmie's birthday, so he insisted that my parents come up with a different name. This was somehow meant to protect me from an untimely death.

It puzzled me that my brother had been named after Dad's best friend who was a naval officer during World War two. Here was a young man who died tragically at an early age and yet, it was considered a wonderful thing to name a child after him. Perhaps it had something to do with the fact he was a war hero. At any rate it seemed that this was another case where the 'rules' were different for men and women. But this was a subject that was not open to debate as Mom and Grampa never spoke of Dad's friend. It was one of a number of forbidden topics that were not to be brought up, especially in Dad's presence.

Another of those forbidden topics was the nightmares I was having. On a regular basis, I would wake up in the middle of the night in a state of terror, certain that I was about to die. It was like waking up in the middle of a movie set in some other time and place. Sometimes it was a bloody battlefield, sometimes the scene of a fire, or other times I was drowning in stormy seas.

When I insisted that these 'bad dreams' were real and I was REALLY there, my Dad would attempt to comfort me by saying that all children have nightmares and there is nothing real about them. Once Dad left the house for work Mom warned me that I mustn't upset my father with any fears that I might die. Dad had seen his little brother get hit by a car when he was a boy, and anything that reminded him of that event would strain his heart.

Whenever I visited my grandfather I used to ask about the photograph of the two boys in his living room, but Grampa wouldn't talk about the little boy who had died.

Overall, I have very fond memories of visiting Grampa Ben's big old house as a child. There were lots of wonderful places to hide when we played my favourite game of 'hide and seek'. Grampa also had a huge prize-winning garden bordering his back yard. I loved the bright splashes of pink peonies and floppy purple iris. Each spring when he planted the annuals, Grampa taught me all the names- snapdragon, lobelia, begonia, nasturtium and zinnia. I was especially proud when he assigned me the task of picking assortments of brightly coloured pansies for the dining room table.

On hot summer days, Grampa made the best lemonade from fresh squeezed lemons. I loved how the lemon slices were magnified through the frosty glass pitcher. We'd have sandwiches garnished with nasturtium from the garden and homemade sugar cookies served on fancy platters. And of course, Grampa would always warn me, 'Girls must never take the last cookie on the plate!' Then we would both dissolve into laughter as we chanted, "Because nobody wants to end up an old maid!!!"

As a youngster, I never thought to question that superstition, nor why it was such a dreadful fate to be 'an old maid.' The message was definitely clear though that marriage was the only respectable state for women and that a woman without a man was somehow deficient. It also did not occur to me to ask why the same stigma did not apply to men. Old Mr. Wilson down the street was a bachelor and nobody seemed to mind that.

In those days, I believed that Dad and Grampa knew

everything. It must be so or they wouldn't be the boss. I learned in Sunday School that God was a 'He' and Jesus, his son was also a 'He'. The minister at church was a 'he' and so were all the religious leaders that I knew of. And God was supposed to be all-knowing so maybe it just fell naturally to men to be the ultimate authorities. At least that's what the bible seemed to say. And my favourite books backed it up, that women were delicate and helpless and needed to be endlessly rescued by princes and knights.

For by far, my most cherished memories of visiting Grampa Ben were the afternoons I spent cuddled into the crook of his arm as he read to me by the hour. We sat together in his big overstuffed chair and read wonderful stories of ogres, gremlins, and knights in shining armour who rescued beautiful damsels in distress. Inevitably the protagonists would fall in love, get married and "live happily ever after." Grampa would then tell me about the days when Granny Bessie was alive and how much he had loved her.

Granny Bessie died of a sudden heart attack when I was only two years old so I had no memory of her. But Grampa made sure I knew about her by showing me the family photographs and telling me the stories of their many adventures. Often he would have a tear in his eye, followed by a bout of chest pain. Then he would reach into his pocket for his nitro-glycerine pills, saying, "I'll be alright in a minute." After offering me a peppermint, he would tell me I must be sure to be a good girl around my father, Frank, as he had a very weak heart and nothing must happen to upset him.

I learned very early in life that heart disease ran in the family. It was strange that none of the characters in my storybooks had heart problems but Dad was still my hero and I preferred not to think about it. I just tried very hard to be a good girl and hoped for the best. But my beloved Dad died of heart failure all the same in 1959 just before my eleventh birthday. Mom was very stoical and put on a brave front that we would manage. No one was allowed to cry.

But Grampa Ben lost it completely. Visits to his house were no longer fun as he slipped into deep depression and denial. It frightened me when he used to telephone Dad's former workplace and got into fights with the receptionist who gently reminded Grampa that his son was deceased. Grampa would fly into a rage and insist that he had seen Dad only that morning at breakfast.

As his hallucinations increased, Grampa became very cantankerous. He absolutely refused to consider moving to a seniors' home. Instead, he hired a housekeeper to look after him and hotly maintained that he wished to die in his own home. Indeed that is what happened. Grampa died peacefully in his sleep one night in 1962.

Grampa Ben had left instructions that he wanted to be laid out at home and that there be a small funeral from the house. The minister came and conducted a short service right in the living room. I remember thinking that Grampa's living room was now a 'dead room' but didn't dare open my mouth to say so. It shocked me that the housekeeper had prepared sandwiches and tea that were served in the dining room right next to where Grampa was laid out. I just couldn't understand how anyone could have an appetite when there was a dead body in the next room.

After the funeral, a real estate agent came to the house and installed a "For Sale" sign in the middle of the front lawn. I had mixed feelings about the sale of the old house. It held so many memories, but not all of them were happy. I saw that people do not "live happily ever after" and I wondered why adults fill children's heads full of lies like that. It had become very clear to me that people get sick and die and are wrenched apart. The happy times are overshadowed by grief and loss and pain.

Some of Dad's cousins came and helped my mother to clear out Grampa's house. One day, Mom came home with an old brown wooden box. She said she had found it in Grampa's attic and that someday it might be of interest to me. It contained some yellowed newspaper clippings as well as a large packet of letters that told the story of Grampa's sister, Emmie, who died in Ireland in 1897. At that time I still hadn't gotten over the death of my father nor of Grampa Ben. The last thing I wanted to do was hear about another death in the family. So the box was put away for some other time.

My brother and I were the beneficiaries of Grampa's estate. But there was a catch. The money was to be left in a Trust Account until we reached the age of twenty-four. Mom was certain that Grampa arranged things that way because he firmly believed that women and children should not have access to money. So there would be no relief in our tight financial situation.

Because of his heart damage, our Dad had been unable to get life insurance. When he died Mom had to go out to work to support us. Women didn't earn much in those days, so Mom was always lamenting that 'the wolf was at the door.' That must be how I picked up the idea that if we spent money, calamity would soon follow.

We children were also saddled with a huge list of responsibilities. I took over all the cooking, grocery shopping, and much of the household cleaning. My brother did the heavy chores like mowing the lawn, shovelling snow, and changing the storm windows every spring and fall. We were still expected to do well in school, so there was little time to play after homework and chores were done.

Certainly, I mark the end of childhood from the time of my father's death. My teenage years were very difficult. Mom and I had never gotten on well and I had lost Dad as an ally. Our relationship worsened as I attempted to assert my independence and express unorthodox beliefs. Fear and denigration were the tactics she continued to use to exert control. Mom regularly expressed her beliefs in doom and gloom. In my young mind, Dad's and Grampa's deaths coupled with our diminished financial status provided ample evidence that our home was darkened by a black storm cloud. Lightening might strike at any time!

Mom was always in a rage about something and I responded by retreating into a state of isolation as a means of self-preservation. When I failed to meet the impossibly high standards she set, especially around housekeeping chores or cooking, there was an inevitable tirade of criticism and nasty name-calling. Before long, I simply believed myself to be inadequate and incapable of doing a good job at anything. Mom's insistence that children were 'just born bad' appeared to be true.

Then there were the practical realities of our situation. While the odd child amongst my peers reported the death of a grandparent, I did not know anyone whose father had died. By age fourteen all of my grandparents were gone. Mom went out to work and assigned to me an unusually heavy load of household chores and responsibilities. Aware that my peers had both parents and much easier lives, I wondered if I had been singled out for some kind of punishment. In those days there was no such thing as grief counselling, nor did anyone step forward to ask how I was coping within a devastated family.

In current times, modern psychology and child-rearing studies are generally in agreement that a child's mind and approach to life are pretty much set by ten years of age. Many years later, I identified several basic mental habits that had been set as a result of the family circumstances into which I had been born. These included the aforementioned storm cloud thinking, low self-esteem and self-isolation. I was very fearful of confrontation, especially when it came to vocalizing my feelings and opinions.

It took many decades for me to see the positive side of a difficult childhood. Extra responsibility and self-reliance cultivated an independent spirit and a notion that I could march to the tune of my own drum. I developed a sense of resourcefulness and was less inclined to take things for granted. I wanted to know what made people tick; why my mother was such an angry person and why Grampa Ben had lost his mind. Life was full of many question marks and I became determined to find answers.

~~~~~

ELEVEN

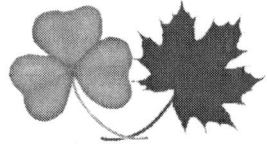

Study Of Life And The Universe

Looking for Answers

Born in the aftermath of war and devastation, my fellow baby boomers and I came of age in the 1960's. We observed the rise of the hippie counterculture and a myriad of groups that opposed political and social orthodoxy. However, there was little time for me to get involved in heady and exciting events like peace marches or rock festivals due to the heavy load of responsibilities I carried with schoolwork and household chores. In spite of a lingering patriarchal atmosphere in our home, my teenage years were strongly influenced by a revolutionary social scene that promoted individual rights, freedom, and self-awareness.

My high school education had been dominated by an awareness of the physical world in traditional subjects such as geometry, chemistry and biology. I developed a fascination for the workings of the human body and considered becoming a doctor. In university, I was introduced to the social sciences and philosophy. World Religions, Anthropology and Sociology opened a whole new wave of questioning. Why do human beings have so many differing and opposing beliefs? What determines the culture into which a person is born? Is one culture better than another and whose religion is right?

Influenced by The Women's Movement, I took for granted that higher education was the right of all women. It infuriated me to learn that there were quotas on how many females versus males could be admitted to medical school. The net result was that women had to work harder and get considerably higher grades than men in order to gain admission. This was a bitter pill to swallow and, rankling at the unfairness, I abandoned my plans to become a doctor.

Instead, I combined university education with nursing school and ultimately became an obstetrical nurse. Being involved with childbirth and new babies was exhilarating! It gave me some much-needed balance in the face of all the deaths that had occurred in my earlier family life. I was overtaken by the desire to experience childbirth on a personal level. This yearning prompted an early marriage and the arrival of two children. Finally, here was something I was good at! Well, the 'children' part went well. Marriage was another matter that wasn't so straightforward. Even with professional counselling, things didn't work out and the marriage ended in divorce when my sons were four and eight years old.

The inevitable distress over a failed marriage led me to a path of self-examination through the study of traditional as well as modern psychology. I took up yoga, attended new-age seminars and joined a women's support team. I went to 'therapy' to learn to come to terms with parental abuses and to deal with unresolved grief. Anything that promised to shed light on how I could possibly be repeating the patterns of my childhood became my focus. For it dawned on me that, like my mother, I had become a single parent who had to work full time to support her children. There was nothing forthcoming initially in the way of child support payments and finances were tight at the best of times. How could history be repeating itself?

Keeping up with the responsibilities of career, marriage, two children, divorce and single parenting was exhausting. I also became a statistic of the "Sandwich Generation" when my kids were teenagers and Mom and her sister developed Alzheimer's disease. The Women's Movement had promised that modern women could have it all. In those days I questioned whether this supposed freedom was all it was cracked up to be.

On the other hand, I had my independence and totally enjoyed watching my boys go through the various stages of growing up and becoming young men. (Today, they are still my pride and joy!) When they were growing up, it worried me that my boys might pick up some of the negative beliefs and self-criticism that I had taken on as a kid. I was determined to do my best to break that cycle of negativity in the hopes that future generations would fare better than I had. My attention therefore focused on the nature of belief and how old falsehoods are handed down from one generation to the next in every culture.

I waded through a plethora of theories on human behaviour from Freud and Jung to the more recent 'New Age' gurus of pop psychology. While authorities in Western psychology had a lot of useful insights to offer, there came a point where I began to turn inward and ask, "What do I believe?" For it was evident that theoretical knowledge of healthy versus unhealthy thought patterns was not sufficient to prevent me from 'defaulting' to old demons of fear of confrontation, low self-esteem and verbal inhibition.

My previous studies in world religions, especially Hinduism and Buddhism, had introduced me to 'Eastern' approaches to the function of the mind. I enrolled in various courses in meditation and mindfulness, initially to help relieve stress. These activities, though often tedious, brought awareness of how my own mind was operating and what life events triggered undesirable emotions and behaviours.

Another phenomenon that occurred in those days was a resurgence of the dreams/nightmares that had been a feature in my childhood. These 'dreams' were different from ordinary ones in that they were much more vivid and emotionally intense. Rather than being a passive observer, I felt a visceral participation in the scenes that surfaced. I felt certain there was a connection between my daytime explorations into the function of the mind and my nightly forays into 'other times and dimensions'.

There were plenty of books around written by people who believed they had lived before in different bodies and historical times. Various researchers attempted to corroborate their stories by verifying the details of the memories they claimed to have. I was more interested in making sense of why we are reborn and what determines our life circumstances. Inevitably, the concept of 'karma' fell into play.

I had thought of karma as a moral and religious doctrine referring to Hindu and Buddhist belief in the transmigration of souls, that is, after death the soul returns to inhabit a new body over and over again. The particular circumstances of each new birth are determined by our actions, good or bad, in previous lifetimes. In view of my difficult childhood, I wondered if my original life circumstances were just random or if there is some order that determined the family into which I had been born. What brought me to a 'WASP' household in Canada as opposed to some extremely different culture in the world? What determined my natural abilities as well as those of my children?

Shift From External to Internal Authority

My younger son had announced when he was five that he 'had been a Buddha man before and that he used to sit and watch the T.V. in his head for hours.' It therefore didn't surprise me when he announced his intention to travel to India and to become a Yoga teacher. My older son had a completely different personality along with a gift for combining art and technology to build or repair just about anything. I considered it a parental duty to nurture and encourage those abilities and to draw out the inner wisdom that was behind them.

Both of my boys had taken Martial Arts lessons as teenagers. Initially, I thought that was only for strong young men but was surprised to see that there were lots of women participating as well. I had heard that Martial Arts can be described as "meditation in action" so I decided to give it a try, starting with Tai Chi.

Curiosity led me to try out the more vigorous practices of Karate and Asian weaponry. I enjoyed observing how the personalities of my fellow classmates were expressed through the physical forms and methods of self-defense. On a personal level, the most prevalent instruction the teacher gave me was "You need to have more faith in yourself!"

I discovered that one of the most beneficial opportunities for mental self-examination lay in learning to defend oneself from physical attack. There were some big men in my classes who took on the role of attackers in simulated fight scenes. Needless to say, this was very intimidating, both mentally and emotionally. (Some of the women could be pretty scary too!)

Over time, as my months of training turned into years, I realized that I could take on the persona of 'one of those scary women' too. I found that my own fears of being harmed did not disappear but that, in the face of fear, I was capable of acting competently to defend myself. I was learning to deal with confrontation and to stand up for myself. At the same time my health was improving greatly with a much lower incidence of colds and other microbial infections. This was first-hand experience of a clear correlation between mental, emotional and physical health.

While it had never been my intention to attain a 'Black Belt', I eventually realized that this was a possibility for me. The most striking thing about it was that my beliefs about who and what I was had been turned upside down. Martial Arts had been a great forum to see how beliefs can be formed or completely changed. The attitudes I had grown up with that women are weak and defenseless were blown out of the water! Through personal experience I saw that the mind is fluid and that truth is, indeed relative.

Martial Arts training challenged my childhood pictures of "the knight in shining armour " as the epitome of strength and heroism. The Samurai, or Japanese knight, was known to have a well-developed intuition. I had always considered that intuition was a female trait associated with the 'weaker sex'. It was a revelation to me that physical agility and intuitive acumen could be equally valued.

Though male in gender, the Samurai warrior acknowledged a 'hidden' feminine strength. I began to attribute strength rather than weakness to my feminine qualities. Of equal merit was the experience that there was a hidden male warrior within my physical female body. Yet, this was something my male instructor could not teach me. A seventeenth century Zen swordsman named Hori Kintayu spoke about this phenomenon:

"The last thing can never be transmitted from one person to another. It comes from within oneself. All the technical discipline is meant to make swordsmen finally see this. It is also the case with learning generally. There is not much use in mere scholarship. You may read all the books there are on the subject of spiritual training and attainment, but the culmination is to realize the mystery of being, and the realization is from within yourself, for it cannot come from anywhere else. If it does, it is not yours but somebody else's."

A major shift in consciousness occurred once I had personal experience that women do not require male protection just because of our gender. My viewpoint altered from identifying with being 'female' to being a person who happens to occupy a female body. I also saw my male counterparts as people who happen to occupy male bodies. We were equal in essence, and men could only be dominant over women when there is co-operation in that scenario.

In spite of the fact that a slight 'Western' woman was an unlikely candidate to become immersed in ancient Samurai fighting traditions, it somehow felt very natural to me. I had a deep appreciation for Japanese culture that in no way had been part of my upbringing. The physical, emotional and intuitive experiences acquired through my training strengthened a belief that I had indeed lived in other times and locations.

Today it is common knowledge that the Samurai practiced meditation and believed in reincarnation and karma. They were extremely loyal to community and family and honoured their ancestors. I realized that I didn't know much about my ancestors, especially on my father's side. So I began to research my family background, eventually discovering huge numbers of people, both dead and alive, with whom I shared common DNA.

Another strong belief got blown out of the water! For, I was not the semi-orphan that I believed myself to be as a child. Thanks to public archives and the Internet, there was a wealth of information to be found about my forbears. Over time I have connected with long lost cousins and we have shared family photographs and stories. As a consequence, my childhood sense of isolation and abandonment disappeared.

The effort that it took to trace my ancestors and connect with living relatives involved physical travel, long hours straining to read old documents at the library, and the frustration of learning to navigate the Internet. (This was a skill that did not come naturally.) The rewards have been well worth it though, especially on an emotional level as I feel a new and exhilarating sense of connection to my family.

At the same time, my Martial Arts training progressed, eventually resulting in the attainment of third degree black belt status. During a particularly strenuous class one day, I pulled a muscle in my lower back. By the next day I was in tremendous pain and could not get out of bed. A friend recommended me to a local chiropractor who was skilled in a technique called 'ART', a form of deep tissue release. One area where the chiropractor focused his treatment was the lower right hip. That area was particularly 'bound up' and was, he believed, contributing to lower back strain.

The treatments were highly beneficial and my back pain began to resolve, though plenty of rest was still required. With extra time on my hands, I finally got around to beginning the laborious task of transcribing grandaunt Emmie's letters. Within a day or two it dawned on me that Emmie had ruptured her appendix and spent the last week of her life in bed. Could it be mere coincidence that I was drawn to work with her letters at a time when I had parallel physical symptoms i.e. extreme pain and tissue damage in the lower right hip area?

I decided it was no coincidence and that there was some sort of universal order at play. While I couldn't say just what was happening, it occurred to me that some major changes had taken place in my worldview. "Things were coming together." There was something about the combination of meditation and mindfulness, martial arts practice, and family reconnection that gave me a newfound sense of confidence and faith in my own judgment. I had contacted an 'Inner Guide' that was wise, protective and reliable.

One of the tasks that Inner Guide seemed to be encouraging was the publication of my grandaunt's letters. I was really enjoying my ancestor's account of her visit to Ireland and the life she lived with her wealthy relatives in Limerick. Having read Frank McCourt's memoir, "Angela's Ashes", I considered that Emmie's story would provide a stark contrast to McCourt's depiction of

Limerick's impoverished society.

After completing the transcripts of Emmie's letters, I had a strong impulse to travel to Ireland and to follow in Emmie's footsteps on a parallel journey. Since I needed to do some research at the National Archives in London, it would be easy to take the train to the West Coast of England where Emmie had landed in 1897. From there I could use Emmie's firsthand accounts to trace her journey while I followed inner guidance in selecting timing and precise locations to visit.

Once in Ireland, I became more closely acquainted with my newfound "Inner Guide". Certainly, my 'encounter' with Willie Woodburn outside the Kilmainham Gaol put me in a space of heeding my emotions and intuition for the remainder of this journey. While I had never seen the streets or buildings of Dublin before, they FELT familiar. I was thrilled to find Uncle Ben's home in Rathmines as well as the old Heuston train station. The knowledge that Emmie had been in the same locations over one hundred years ago increased my sense of emotional connection to her.

My original itinerary included a plan to stay at a B&B in central Limerick. However, there were no vacancies there so I went along with the advice of a booking agent to stay at a place called 'Clifton House'. I arrived in Limerick on a rainy night and took a cab to that destination. In the extreme darkness, it was impossible to see that this building had been known as Clifton Ville in 1897. It just happened to be in the immediate vicinity of the homes previously owned by the Cleeve families. After a good night's sleep, I awoke to find myself within a short walking distance of the North Circular Road, Bracken Brae, and Sunville.

Furthermore, was it mere coincidence that I met a woman on the street who happened to be a good friend of the current owners of Sunville House? That woman was kind enough to introduce me to her friend and I was graciously offered a tour of the house. Once again, feeling and intuition took over. Somehow, I recognized that some changes had occurred and that the doorway to the "bachelor's quarters" that Emmie spoke of had been walled off. My hostess informed me that that wing of the home had been converted into an apartment in later years.

As we continued on the tour, I was shown the bathroom and master bedroom. My attention was drawn, however, to a bedroom on my right. The goose bumps that appeared on my arms told me that this was the room where Emmie had died. Paradoxically, there was also a sense of warmth in the house and I felt sure that Emmie had enjoyed much of her stay in the Cleeve's home.

After taking my leave of Sunville House and progressing along the North Circular Road, I passed Beechlawn but did not stop in. Instead I moved on and located Fernbank which is now occupied by the Salesian nuns and has undergone extensive renovations. I had a visit in the old front parlour with one of the nuns who was very kind to photocopy some news articles on the history of the house. She allowed me to photograph a water colour painting of the home as it had appeared in 1897.

My next stop down the road was the Condensed Milk Manufactory, now known as Golden Vale Creamery. I learned that the political and class strife known as 'The Troubles' along with the rise of trade unionism in Ireland resulted in bankruptcy for the business House of Cleeve by 1923. Thomas Cleeve had been knighted in 1900 and died just eight years later. His son Frank eventually took over the business but left Ireland after the collapse and liquidation of the company. It dawned on me that if Emmie had married Frank Cleeve she would have gone through very wrenching experiences during those troubled times.

My last stop of the day was the graveyard at St. Mary's Cathedral. The descriptions in Cousin Mary's letters helped to locate Emmie's gravestone. I wondered once again if it was just coincidence that it began to rain as I contemplated the tragedy of Emmie's untimely demise. With tears streaming down my face, it felt as though 'Mother Nature' had joined me in expressing our sadness.

It took some doing to get my head around being both dead and alive. This stone monument told me that Emmie was dead, but I believed that her essence had continued on and had returned to Ireland in the body now occupied by me. I had the benefit of forty more years of living than Emmie had. Unimaginable social change had occurred since 1897. I was now free to give voice to the thoughts and desires that Emmie had not dared to express so long ago. I somehow felt that I owed it to her to tell her story and made a solemn promise to do so.

That evening, back at Clifton House, I meditated on the strange inner feeling I'd had at Emmie's grave. Thinking in terms of karma, perhaps it was my destiny to make this trip to Ireland. Karma no longer felt like an exotic religious belief or an externally imposed dogma. In a very secular way, karma felt real to me because I was having experiences on an inner level that confirmed its truth.

Karma

Over time I reflected on Emmie's life and identified what I believed her karma to be. Her greatest desire at the time of her death had been to return to her family in Canada. If only she had sought medical attention, she could have had life-saving surgery. If only she had spoken up for herself and made it clear that she had no interest in marriage. If only – not much use in following that line of thinking. Emmie died. It's too late to change that. Perhaps it would be more useful to identify the factors that prevented Emmie from taking the steps that could have resulted in her living a full lifespan.

Given that the definition of the word 'karma' is simply 'action', Emmie's karma can be deduced through the behaviour she revealed in her letters. That is, there were some actions that Emmie took and several she failed to take that could have resulted in a different outcome. Scrutiny of the letters led me to conclude that, at the time of her death, Emmie was restricted by the following mental habits and associated emotions:

1) Negative self assessment
2) Self isolation
3) Storm cloud thinking
4) Fear of confrontation
5) Inability to speak up on her own behalf

In my view, all of these factors were expressions of a deep underlying sense of powerlessness that played out in different ways.

Negative Self Assessment

Evidence of low self esteem shows up in several places in Emmie's letters. When she replied to her brother, Edward, regarding his question about finding a mate, she said, "There must be something wrong in my composition, for I cannot get along with young men." No one in her family supported a view that women ought to have a choice about whether or not they married. In the face of overwhelming opposition, what else could she conclude but that there must be something wrong with her?

In those days, obedience to parents was a strong measure of whether one was a good person or not. While it is true that Willie and Bel had sent Emmie to Ireland for the purpose of finding a suitable mate, they had not banished her from the family. They would have been quite happy to have her return to Canada and settle down with whichever young man she had chosen in Ireland. However, Emmie concluded that she had been turned out. Lacking faith in her own value, she projected that her parents no longer found her worthy.

Further evidence of self-doubt can be gleaned from a defensive mechanism that Emmie used to tell her parents that she was considered by others in a positive light: "Cousin Phoebe sends you her love and says to say that you have brought me up well, that I am a good child, and very useful and that she is very fond of me. Mr. Fogarty and Mrs. Baylor agreed that I was a very nice, clever, useful girl. The Cleeve brothers and Jack Boyd made so many remarks that I was the colour of my rose." One has to ask why Emmie felt it necessary to reinforce to her own parents that she was 'a good girl'.

If Emmie had somehow been magically transported back home to Canada nothing would have really changed. Emmie still saw herself as a single woman. Her family saw her as a wife who had not yet reached her potential. She had not factored in that her relatives' comments were based on her potential as a married woman and were NOT about her as a single and complete person.

In retrospect, I answered my childhood question about why it was acceptable for a man to be a bachelor but not for a woman to remain a spinster. Men could be seen to reach their potential through their occupation and the income they earned. Most women didn't earn an income then and the only reputable occupation for women was that of wife and mother. Unmarried women were considered powerless, and therefore, had not met their potential.

Self Isolation

Perhaps as a result of the pressures she was subjected to in Ireland, Emmie distanced herself from her relatives. No doubt she felt misunderstood and that she dare not give voice to her inner convictions about marriage. Maybe the only way that Emmie could remain internally true to herself was to erect a false construct that her Irish relatives were not really 'family': "I want my mother to coddle me. I have no one here although all are very kind. I am afraid I would not like being coddled by any but my own people."

The veiled pressures that were exerted on Emmie through teasing and innuendo led to feelings of embarrassment and shame. Maybe this is another reason why Emmie did not consider herself 'one of the family' amongst her Irish relatives. Rather than accept herself as an independent spirit, Emmie decided that there was something wrong with her distaste for her male contemporaries. Her rejection of Frank's marriage proposal must be evidence of some deep lack of gratitude. Every other young woman in Limerick would have jumped at the chance to marry Frank Cleeve! What ever was wrong with Emmie Woodburn?

In truth, there was nothing wrong with Emmie. She was entitled to her likes and dislikes and to choose the course of her life. But she cannot be blamed for not seeing it that way in 1897. In the absence of external support for her point of view, Emmie's inner conviction was just not strong enough to do battle with her entire family. With no one to back her up, Emmie considered herself a stranger in the Cleeve household.

Obviously, the love of family was highly important to Emmie. She wanted to maintain a positive reputation as a guest in the Cleeve homes. Generally she subscribed to their values and principles with ONE exception: Emmie wanted no part of marriage. She had only two options – to conform to her relatives' expectations or to rebel. Her inability to take action in one direction or the other left her powerless.

Storm Cloud Thinking

In their letters after Emmie's death, both cousins Mary Boyd and Phoebe Cleeve made a point of stating that Emmie had passed off her 'hip pains' as minor and she had not asked to consult a doctor. No one considered that her condition was serious nor that Emmie was avoiding incurring any expense on her behalf. Cousin Mary did not pick up on the significance of Emmie's statement that "Something very bad was hanging over her." On an inner level, Emmie knew she was in danger but her warning was not heeded – her feelings of doom were dismissed as silly and unfounded.

Emmie was also unduly worried about her family. She frequently expressed concern for her mother's health and seemed not to accept Bel's assurances that she was quite fine. Willie was solving his employment and financial issues in his own way. Emmie's presence was not required to 'help' her father to sort things out. But Emmie didn't see it that way and worried unnecessarily that her parents were headed for further disasters. As a result, she was not able to relax and enjoy her stay in Ireland, thus compounding the stress she was feeling over the 'marriage issue'.

Fear of Confrontation

Emmie was not one to address issues head-on. Once she thought that her father had turned her out due to their financial losses, Emmie did not come right out and ask him if that was in fact the case. Instead she attempted to ingratiate herself to her father and presented a plan to deal with family finances:

"I do so love to get home letters, and dear Dad, I am so pleased you have work. Even if the pay is not all it might be, it may lead to better. If we were together –and I pray that will be soon- if Edward and Dick boarded with us we could live on $600 if we were economical, which dear Mother is. Soon Harry will be earning, and then there will be only three of us to look after."

Emmie did not take her parents to task for their failure to let her know they expected her to find a mate in Ireland. There is no evidence in her letters that she had talked to anyone in Ireland about her suspicions that there was a conspiracy afoot:

"She (Mary) is very anxious to see me well dressed. I think she wants to get me married while I am in Ireland. In fact I think all my relations do, much to my amusement. They expect me to have a good time in August when the young people are home and the house is to be full of visitors."

Rather than flatly declare her personal wish to return to Canada, Emmie clouded her plea by suggesting that both father and mother must need her to look after them:

"I do miss you and Mother so! I wonder if you think of me more on Sunday than on other days; for I never seem to forget you all that day, even for a moment. How is Mother looking? Is she able to get along alone? You know I can go home any time I am needed."

"Be sure and tell me every time you write how you are and if you want me to go home. Remember I will go any day you send for me....I am Mother's girl and will not leave my home unless Father turns me out."

There was no power in Emmie's voice when she beat about the bush and offered vague suggestions about her value as a useful servant. She betrayed an underlying fear that she was stuck in Ireland and that her fate rested entirely with the good will of her wealthy relatives.

Inability to Speak up on Her Own Behalf

Emmie's letters suggest that she felt closest to her cousin Mary Boyd. Mary was the youngest amongst the Cleeve children and, like Emmie, was the only girl. Perhaps the two cousins felt a special bond as a result. Mary did try to appeal to her brother Tom to 'ease up' on Emmie but she wasn't willing to go the distance once Tom got angry about Emmie's stubbornness. He was the family patriarch and his word was law. None of the Cleeve women dared cross him so Mary knew that no one else would back her up. They had all bought into the prevailing social order that accepted male domination.

Emmie well knew that this was the case. She likely did not wish to be the cause for upset within the Cleeve family. Because she valued peace and harmony, Emmie chose to put a lid on her inner rebellion and kept her resentments to herself. That energy had to go somewhere. Some would say that her ruptured appendix was a physical manifestation of her unspoken anger. There was a lot that Emmie was not saying!

Emmie wasn't different from most women in Victorian times. Generally speaking, women were expected to be compliant, sweet natured and silent. Decision-making and the voicing of opinions were male prerogatives. Emmie's status as a guest and female underling stripped her of any power to speak up on her own behalf.

Given that we don't exist in a vacuum, there was probably little Emmie could do for herself in her social and cultural milieu. The times had not yet caught up to respect the wishes of a woman who wanted to remain unmarried. It was still very much a 'man's world' and independent women were either unappreciated or looked upon with suspicion. These were the circumstances, both personal and social, that marked the end of Emmie's lifetime. Perhaps it would take an environment that was more open and supportive for Emmie to resolve her conflict.

Emmie made a strong effort to conform. But somewhere deep within there was a powerful energy that just could not buy into the social views of her time. Not surprisingly, she was caught in a great web of confusion and fear. Emmie could not find the lamp that would lead her out of the darkness. The time had not yet come when 'ordinary people' scrutinized their beliefs and where they came from.

Making Sense of My Childhood

Some people believe that there is no particular explanation for our birth circumstances. They would say that our cultural background and milieu occurs randomly. Others would say that whether rich or poor, we all suffer from painful or difficult life circumstances. They might even say that this is due to the meting out of 'divine punishment'. As a child, I often felt that I had been unfairly singled out for punishment. Frightened of my mother, I was constantly on the lookout for the next physical or verbal attack. The losses of my father and grandfather were devastating. Financial reverses also added to a high stress load.

In the face of adversity it is very human to ask 'why' or 'why me'. In retrospect, I believe that it was the hardships of my childhood that largely shaped my personality. However, it is also evident that different people react to adversity (or good fortune) in many different ways.

Some people develop a rebellious streak; others succumb to addictions, while some are spurred on to overcome adversity through the relentless pursuit of success. There appears to be an inner pattern with which each of us is born. In our youth, most of us just don't have conscious awareness of what that pattern is nor that it may be guiding us in a particular direction.

Considering my current lifetime, I note that my formative self-concepts were not much different from Emmie's. By age ten I had absorbed a belief that I was just born bad. My identity was tied up in being female and less desirable than my male contemporaries. On a societal level, men certainly seemed to me to be in charge.

But there was one thing that had definitely changed. That lamp that Emmie could not find was burning brightly for me. Thanks to 'The Women's Movement' and the courageous actions of a growing number of people, a full education was open to me. I was free to attend university where I focused on the study of human behaviour. Subjects such as sociology, psychology and comparative religion became 'soul food' as I delved into the mysteries of what makes people tick.

I have come to believe that it is significant that I was born on Emmie's birthday. It has also been a wonderful gift to inherit her letters. My inner experiences while studying those letters in depth resulted in the realization that Emmie and I (Liz) are similar in temperament. Identifying significant aspects of Emmie's state of mind at the time of her death helped me to come up with answers to my childhood questions as to why I had been born into my particular family.

Considering the notion of karma, it made sense to me that there must have been past life tendencies that I needed to improve upon. It was not a matter of punishment or inherent sinfulness. Instead, it felt right that I had been born into a family that provided the circumstances necessary for me to move on from past negativity. A more secular approach to the term 'karma' was more palatable to me than a religious notion of Divine Retribution.

I was born to a mother who did not like children and who lacked good parenting skills. She instilled a belief that children are born bad and deserve to be punished. (As if that would help!) The death of my father and lack of grief counselling left me with strong feelings of abandonment and unworthiness.

By the age of fourteen, I was reeling from the loss of my father and all of my grandparents. My brother left home and Mom did little to stay connected with my paternal relatives. At the level of family, I felt 'cut off'. There was not much time to socialize, at least not as often as other kids did. This left me feeling very different.

As children, my brother and I walked on eggshells. Between Mom's angry outbursts and Dad's fragile health, we were well motivated to avoid calamity. It seemed that a dark cloud hung over our home predicting impending doom. Life provided ample evidence that this was the case with the successive losses of our loved ones.

Fear of confrontation and the failure to use my voice were, therefore, prime features of my early life. Low self esteem contributed to a sense that I was not worthy of having a say in what happened to me. All of these factors contributed to a sense of isolation and lack of faith in myself or in the good will of others.

Once I compared my formative traits to Emmie's state of mind at the time of her death, I saw a match. This view allowed me to move away from feeling victimized towards the acceptance that my prior life actions had determined my current life circumstances. Not only that, it was not a matter of 'crime and punishment', but one of changing my self-definition and learning to accept myself as an inherently good and capable human being.

It became easier to acknowledge that there were many positive traits in my basic make-up. These included a tendency to question and seek innovative ways of thinking. I recognized a genuine sense of caring for people and a strong desire to contribute. Sometimes a sense of humour jumped out along with a love of children and animals.

Affirming Ordinary Wisdom

I was never aware of any pre-set plan when it comes to the activities I became involved with over the course of my life. Some proponents of reincarnation say that there is a period in between lifetimes when an individual reviews the past and agrees to accept specific life circumstances for the next lifetime. I cannot claim any consciousness of such a situation. What I can confirm is the connection over time with "Inner Guidance" that is wise and purposeful. Because this is an inner process, and therefore highly personal, no one else can do the work for us, but each of us has this same inner capacity.

I believe that it was this "Inner Guide" that led me to train in martial arts where I learned to deal with confrontation and how to act effectively in the face of fear. (Not that I enjoy it, mind you. But after eighteen years of training, I can speak up for myself when the situation warrants it.) In short, I learned to rescue myself.

Like a nurturing mother, this Inner Guide knew that I needed to shed my sense of being orphaned and to reconnect with family. I had not planned to study my family history. It was an unrelated research project that led me to the public archives and a complete surprise when I came across information about my father's family. One thing led to another and I have succeeded in locating a number of long lost cousins. What a joy this has been!

In terms of timing, there has not been any highly ordered and sequential lesson plan to my life. Looking back over the past sixty years, I am beginning to pull together the threads and common themes of my existence. Reflection upon the major life activities to which I have been attracted has resulted in the conclusion that there is wisdom inherent in our desires and leanings. That is, we are attracted to life situations that teach us about our true nature and that ultimately enhance our connection to all of life.

One thing I am clear about is that I could not have written this book any earlier in my life. Many diverse experiences contributed to my getting here. It has been vitally important to move beyond a theoretical belief in reincarnation to one that is internally experienced. I have also needed to develop faith in myself and to find the courage to speak up.

That being said, it is not my aim to convince anyone of 'my truths'. The most I can do is to share my story and invite people to seek out their own inner wisdom. The pathway will look different for each of us. I encourage everyone to question their beliefs and where they came from. Do I really believe 'this or that' or have I absorbed beliefs from external sources that are not truly mine?

"Emmie Returns" has been presented as "a memoir of two lifetimes" in order to demonstrate how one lifetime flows into the next. Initially, I had considered that my grandaunt's story provided an interesting glimpse of life for women in the Victorian era. It felt quite safe to report on four months of someone else's life. Once I came to the conclusion that Emmie and I are two aspects of the same Being, everything changed. This was no longer someone else's life that was put on public display. Emmie's story had become my story and I felt totally naked in exposing my belief in reincarnation along with the experiences that led to that conclusion.

My dilemma was resolved through returning to a self-assessment of inherent goodness. Included in that identity is acknowledgement of an inner wisdom even if I am not always in touch with it. Sometimes fear and pain block the connection. As human beings, we benefit one another by sharing our life stories and how we solve problems. People are free to believe what they like and to take whatever is useful from those stories.

Emmie's letters provide a first hand account of much of what was going on in the mind of one human being whose life was cut short. I suspect Emmie would have been very surprised to learn that in a hundred years time, her life story would become available for the whole world to read. In many ways, it is just as much a surprise for me to expose a lifetime of trial and error in this lifetime. Quite frankly, I'd rather enjoy the comfort of anonymity.

But that is not my karmic mission. Through very personal struggles to find and use my voice, I desire to offer my experience to others in the same predicament. As a child, my behaviour was governed by a belief that one had to be an acknowledged authority to have anything valid to say. As a young adult, I considered myself an ordinary human being, separate from the community of scholars and advisors who ought to be listened to.

What authority do I have to ask people to consider that we have lived other lifetimes? The so-called authority I was standing upon was based on evidence that would be considered flimsy at best, and downright unbelievable at worst. I became a bundle of fear and confusion, desperately trying to come up with an explanation to validate my experience.

Contemplation on the matter took me back to my childhood when I tried so hard to convince my father that my nightmares of dying in other times and places were real and I had REALLY been there. And what about that experience I had on the misty pathway in Dublin? That was prompted by intuition and strong emotion followed by what some might call a 'vision'.

Eureka! The lights had just turned on. All of my experiences that pointed toward affirming that Emmie and I are one and the same soul were expressions of 'feminine energy'. While women have made great strides in attaining egalitarian status with men, those expressions of feminine energy that are the underpinnings of this story are generally not validated in today's world of hard science.

In scientific experiments, we turn our attention outward and measure what can be seen with our vision, hearing and sense of touch. As such, these can be referred to as activities that are 'masculine' in nature. Emmie's story is about information gained by turning our attention inward to find an inner wisdom that is feminine in its nature. No wonder I was frightened to claim that information gained through methods not discernable to the eyes and ears was valid and intelligent. But I assert that these are capacities that everyone has and they can be accessed by anyone willing to acknowledge their existence and value.

So Emmie and I have come full circle. In 1897 she struggled to affirm her value as a single female. Today, my situation as Liz is essentially the same in my efforts to affirm 'feminine energy' as wise and valid. In 1897 Emmie failed to speak up on her own behalf. At the time of her death, she had succumbed to the fear and confusion that were the by-products of conflict between her inner and outer world. A hundred years later, I have reached the same fork in the road.

Should I maintain the safety of silence or should I take the uncomfortable risk of speaking up? Emmie didn't fare so well by keeping silent. Both she and her family suffered through her untimely death. Emmie might well have created a different ending to her story if she had taken a stand for her right to choose the life she desired.

I compare our situation to that of the driver of a car whose vehicle breaks down on the road to a destination. We have the option to obtain another vehicle and carry on with the journey. Today, as Liz, I regret that we still live in a world where far too many people, especially women, do not have the right to self-determination. Who knows what impact the words of one person can make? Those of us who can speak up, MUST!

Acknowledgements

In the final chapters of Emmie Returns, I offered my explanation of how Karma operates from one lifetime to another. Five negative behavioural habits were identified that have required the love and support of other people for me to overcome. This book could not have materialized without the contributions of the many people with whom I share karmic bonds. It is a pleasure to use my voice to express gratitude to the following people:

I thank my parents, Frank Woodburn and Frances MacBeth for creating the physical vehicle that has served me for over sixty years. In spite of a difficult and often painful life, my mother provided the example of staying the course over the long haul. (She lived for nearly one hundred years.) Conceived on my father's birthday, I received the benefit of being treated like a much-appreciated gift by my Dad. His unconditional love has sustained me even though it was our destiny to be together for only a short time.

I thank my Granny Bessie who welcomed me enthusiastically for being a girl, and my Grampa Ben for the hours he spent reading to me as a child, thereby instilling a love for books and storytelling. I barely knew my maternal grandparents, Fred MacBeth and Lizzie Burrows, but I thank them for the family continuity they provided through my maternal lineage.

I especially thank my sons, Aaron and Noah Woods for the joy they have consistently brought into my life. Their unconditional love and support keeps me going through thick and thin. I thank them also for the two fabulous women, Stephanie and Heather, who they have brought into the family.

There have been key people beyond my immediate family, that have assisted me to eradicate the barriers to success in my life:

I thank my instructor, Sensei Martin O'Connell, director of High Park Martial Arts in Toronto for his patience and insistence that I develop faith in myself. He has been instrumental in teaching me to apply the practical elements of confronting opposition in the face of fear as well as in releasing my stifled voice. I am grateful for the atmosphere provided at High Park Martial Arts and thank my Black Belt colleagues, both male and female, for their physical help and camaraderie.

Through their professional guidance, four powerful women have had particular impact in my finding strength in 'feminine energy':

I thank Josephine Newman who assisted me to gain practical coping skills, enjoyment of the little things in life and to acknowledge my accomplishments.

I thank Laura Alden Kamm for her work in "Intuitive Wellness" and for demonstrating her skill in applying the female attributes of intuition and clairvoyance during a recent illness.

I thank Lama Tsultrim Allione for her scholarship in writing "Women of Wisdom" and for her work in translating ancient Buddhist teachings for those of us who have grown up in the West. In 2008 Tsultrim gave me a much-needed gift during a retreat by personally facilitating my deeper connection with the force of compassion.

I thank Julie M. Kramer for her work in Shamanic Journeying.

Julie was instrumental in pointing out the 'unseen agents' that are supporting me to speak up about power as it expresses through the female form. Her encouragement around the concept of this book is greatly appreciated.

Specifically related to the production of this book, I am extremely grateful to Jannine Cox for providing her IT expertise in the building of the Companion Website. Jannine identified and handled an incredible number of tasks throughout all the phases of preparing the manuscript and cover designs for both print and e-publication. Bravo Jannine!

For editorial assistance I thank Margaret Kohr, Caryn Katz and Heather Elson. Each of them has offered astute observations and helpful suggestions beyond their keen-eyed scouring for grammatical errors and typos. What a team!

For additional computer and IT support I thank Stephanie Hunter and Diane Battler. I wouldn't have had the means to create this book without their computer set-up and ongoing consultation. (I also thank Diane for her example as one of the gutsiest martial artists I have ever met!)

I thank Dave Battler, photographer, for making me 'look good' on the Companion Website, in spite of my being cold, wet and cranky during martial arts photo shoots. On the opposite end of the weather spectrum, thank you for coming out in a heat wave to capture my contemporary photo in 'author persona'.

Thanks go to Margaret Pas and Carlos Pereira who contributed their design skills to the book cover and website graphics respectively. Your time and effort are much appreciated.

While Emmie Returns is predominantly a book about finding Internal Authority, there are some authors I wish to acknowledge for the external contribution they have made to my life journey. Their names and some of their works are included in the Book Lists in Appendix A.

In closing, I thank the author of the Koan, "You have to do it by yourself and you cannot do it alone." Reflection on this paradox has inspired me to identify what I need to receive and what I have to give to others in the world.

~~~~~

Appendix A

Selected Bibliography

Books Pertaining to Reincarnation

Bernstein, Morey, *The Search for Bridey Murphy*, Doubleday, Garden City, N.Y., 1965.

Bowman, Carol, *Return from Heaven,* Harper Collins, New York, 2001.

Bowman, Carol, *Children's Past Lives,* Bantam Books, New York, 1997.

Clow, Barbara Hand, *Eye of the Centaur*, Bear and Company Pub., New Mexico, 1986.

Cockell, Jenny, *Across Time and Death- A Mother's Search for her Past Life Children,* Simon & Schuster, New York, 1994.

Cockell, Jenny, *Journeys Through Time,* Piatkus, London, 2009.

Cockell, Jenny, *Past Lives, Future Lives*, Piatkus, London, 1996.

Gershom, Yonasan, *Beyond the Ashes,* A.R.E. Press, Virginia, 1992.

Gershom, Yonasan, *From Ashes to Healing,* A.R.E. Press, Virginia, 1996.

Leininger, Bruce and Andrea, *Soul Survivor*, Grand Central Publishing, New York, 2009.

Linn, Denise, *Past Lives, Present Miracles,* Hay House, California, 2008.

Myss, Caroline, *Sacred Contracts : Awakening Your Divine Potential,* Harmony Books, New York, 2001.

Moody, Raymond A., *Life After Life*, Harper, San Francisco, 2001.

Roberts, Jane, *The Seth Material,* New Awareness Network, New York, 2001.

Stearn, Jess, *Edgar Cayce, The Sleeping Prophet*, Bantam Books, Toronto, 1968.

Stevenson, Ian, *Children who Remember Previous Lives*, University Press of Virginia, Charlottesville, 1987.

Stevenson, Ian, *Twenty Cases Suggestive of Reincarnation*, 2nd. Ed., University Press of Virginia, Charlottesville, 1974.

Svoboda, Robert, *Aghora III: The Law of Karma,* Sadhana Publications, Bellingham, WA, 2000.

Weiss, Brian L., *Many Lives, Many Masters*, Simon & Schuster, New York, 1988.

Weiss, Brian, *Through Time Into Healing,* Fireside, 1993.

Weiss, Brian, *Only Love is Real, A Story of Soulmates Reunited,* Warner Books, New York, 1997.

Woodward, Mary Ann, *Edgar Cayce's Story of Karma,* Coward-McCann, New York, 1971.

Other Useful Books

Allione, Tsultrim, *Feeding Your Demons, Ancient Wisdom for Resolving Inner Conflict,* Little, Brown & Co., New York, 2008.

Allione, Tsultrim, *Women of Wisdom,* Snow Lion publications, New York, 2000.

Christ, Carol, *Diving Deep and Surfacing: Women Writers on a Spiritual Quest,* Beacon Press, Boston, 1980.

Christ, C., & Plaskow, J. (eds.), *Womanspirit Rising: A Feminist Reader in Religion,* Harper & Row, New York, 1979.

Estes, Clarissa P., *Women Who Run With the Wolves,* Ballantine Books, New York, 1992.

Guarneri, Mimi, M.D., *The Heart Speaks, Touchstone,* New York, 2007.

Hay, Louise, *You Can Heal Your Life,* Hay House Inc., California, 1984.

Jampolsky, Gerald, *Love is Letting Go of Fear,* Celestial Arts, Berkeley, 2004.

Jung, Carl, *Memories, Dreams, Reflections,* Vintage Books, New York, 1989.

Kamm, Laura A., *Intuitive Wellness, using your body's inner wisdom to heal,* Atria Books, New York, 2006.

King, Winston L., *Zen and the Way of the Sword, Arming the Samurai Psyche,* Oxford University Press, U.K., 1993.

Kopp, Sheldon, *If You Meet the Buddha on the Road, Kill Him*, Bantam Books, Toronto, 1976.

Lee, David & Jacobs, Debbie, (eds.), *Made in Limerick*, Limerick Civic Trust, 2003.

Lowinsky, Naomi R., *Stories from the Motherline*, J.P. Tarcher, Los Angeles, 1992.

Myss, Caroline, *Anatomy of the Spirit*, Three Rivers Press, New York, 1996.

McCourt, Frank, *Angela's Ashes: A Memoir*, Scribner, New York, 1996.

Northrup, Christiane, M.D., *Women's Bodies, Women's Wisdom*, Revised Ed., Bantam Books, New York, 1998.

Perera, S.B., *Descent to the Goddess: A Way of Initiation for Women*, Inner City Books, Toronto, 1981.

Pert, Candace, *Everything You Need to Know to Feel Go(o)d*, Hay House, California, 2006.

Ray, Reginald, *Touching Enlightenment, Finding Realization in the Body*, Sounds True, Boulder, Colorado, 2008.

Spellissy, Sean, *The History of Limerick*, The Celtic Bookshop, Limerick, 1998.

Suzuki, Daisetz, *Zen and Japanese Culture*, Princeton University Press, New Jersey, 1970.

Suzuki, Shunryu, *Zen Mind, Beginner's Mind*, Weatherhill, New York & Tokyo, 1970.

Svoboda, Robert, *Aghora at the Left Hand of God*, Sadhana Publications, Bellingham WA, 1999.

Taylor, Jill Bolte, *My Stroke of Insight*, Viking, New York, 2008.

Trungpa, Chogyam, *Cutting Through Spiritual Materialism*, Shambhala, Berkeley, 1973.

Trungpa, Chogyam, *The Myth of Freedom*, Shambhala, Berkeley, 1973.

Trungpa, Chogyam, *Born in Tibet*, Shambhala, Boston, 1995

~~~~~

Connect With Me Online

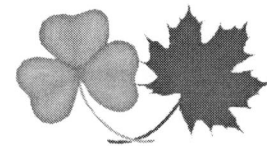

Emmie Returns companion website:
www.woodlandstream.com.
I have created a companion website to my book, Emmie Returns – A Memoir of Two Lifetimes. Along with Emmie's letters, I was especially fortunate to have inherited numerous old family photographs which are on the website, as well as a map of the North Circular road, the family genealogy chart, pictures of Limerick in 1897 and more.

Visit my Facebook page:
www.facebook.com/emmie.returns
Click "Like" to become a fan and stay connected.

About the Author

Born in 1948 in Montreal, Liz Woodburn joined the ranks of the Baby Boom Generation. Her formal education includes university studies in Comparative Religion and the Social Sciences. Liz has pursued a life long informal education through the study of psychology and human behaviour, alternative health care, and various New Age studies. Liz is a regular practitioner of Tai Chi, Chi Gong, meditation and mindfulness. Over the years, Liz has worn the hats of Nurse, Mother, Genealogist and Martial Artist. She currently holds third degree Black Belts in Karate and Traditional Asian Weaponry. Combining a spirit of adventure with a lifetime of 'inner exploration', Liz has now reinvented herself as an author.

Emmie Returns traces the development of Liz's belief in reincarnation through the celebration and validation of feminine energy and wisdom. As an expression of inner power and authority, Liz has chosen to self-publish both in print and e-Book versions, thereby demonstrating a passage from post war Baby Boomer to modern self-determined Zoomer.